NATURE'S WAYS

Nature's Ways

Experiencing the Sacred
in the Natural World

To Jane —
Go in peace
with the Earth.

[signature]

Philip Sutton Chard

To order additional copies of this book, contact:
Xlibris Corporation
1-888-795-4274
www.Xlibris.com
Orders@Xlibris.com
60208

To my beloved children, Daniel and Kira

Acknowledgements

Cover photo: Philip Sutton Chard
Author photo: Cynthia Hines

CONTENTS

INTRODUCTION

Be careful how you interpret the world. It is like that.
—Erich Heller

There are two ways to live your life. One is as though nothing is a miracle. The other is as though everything is a miracle.
—Albert Einstein

It was a crackling-hot August day at a family picnic in rural Illinois. A mere nine-year-old, I was the youngest in attendance and thoroughly bored with the adult conversation, so once I'd had my fill of burgers, corn on the cob, and baked beans, I slipped away and wandered toward the lakeshore where a cooler breeze beckoned. Accompanied by a child's constant companion—imagination—I settled on my back in the lush, moist grass of our backyard. Actually, it was more clover and dandelions than grass, as this era preceded the age of herbicidal lawns. But it was large and open, affording an expansive view of the summer afternoon sky with all the billowing cumulus clouds that are the stuff of pastoral paintings and, through the eyes of a child, of fantastical and morphing shapes.

After a few minutes, I was joined by my godfather, Dennis Cavanaugh, a lanky Irishman who, in his retirement, had amused himself by making violins in his garage, and not very good ones at that. Mr. Cavanaugh was a gifted storyteller who regularly appeared at our house, often on Saturday evenings, to regale and horrify the neighborhood children with tall tales of wolves in the north woods on moonlight nights and of apparitions ghosting past the broken windows of abandoned farmhouses. Decades later and long after his passing, I have come to regard the man as something of a mystic in his own right, although that label was never applied to him. That concept simply wasn't part of the nomenclature in my small farming community.

What's more, he seemed to take the role inherent in his title—godfather—seriously, although he was anything but somber about it. I don't recall him preaching to me, pointing a bony finger at my face to emphasize a point of morality, or otherwise imposing dogma or religious admonitions on my young psyche. Rather, his visits with me were always tinged with enchantment. While most of the adults in my presence were speaking in prose (and mighty stale prose at that), Mr. Cavanaugh always sounded poetic, imaginative, and patiently tolerant of the ambiguity inherent in life's mystery. And although he didn't tell me what to do or how to think, he did urge me in his own oblique, shadowy way to find, trust, and follow my intuition.

And that's what he was doing that steamy summer afternoon as we settled on our backs together, feeling the grass grow itchy against our skin. Before long and without needing to make note of it, we were contemplating the cottony white, gray, and sometimes-murky charcoal of the burgeoning clouds overhead. And although I had no notion at the time, we were awaiting a pivotal lesson in my spiritual life, an opening to nature's ways. In one guise or another, it is a lesson that instructs virtually every human who, by chance or intention, comes into close and meaningful interaction with the natural world.

It began when my godfather spoke, as he often did, by asking a question.

"What do you see?" he queried, motioning toward the sky.

My eyes hopscotched from cloud to cloud, squinting as I circled round toward the blazing sun, now poking from behind a small ball of "cotton" that seemed to be chasing after a bigger one.

"That one's an owl," I pointed. "And there's a bowl of mash potatoes with a dab of butter on top. This up here is a werewolf's head with his claws at the side. That was a speedboat a minute ago, but now it's more like a dragon."

"Oh, I see. I like those," he said with genuine delight.

Another silence settled over us, and in its spaces a new and unwelcome thought crept into my fledgling psyche. It came whispering in one of those shadowy inner voices that scurries like an insect beneath your covers as you sleep. You don't notice until it bites.

"Just clouds," the dry, matter-of-fact voice in my mind whispered, and I twitched a bit as if stung.

"Those are just clouds," it came again in a dour monotone.

And the owl, potatoes, dragons, and metamorphosing shapes vanished right before my sight, replacing what had been imaginatively enchanting with what was intellectually abstract. I rubbed my eyes a few times, blinking, and then shook my head, hoping to summon back the seeing that had just escaped me. But the magical forms had vanished, and struggle as I did, I could not resurrect them.

It was then that Mr. Cavanaugh propped himself up on one elbow, looking down at me through his rose-colored glasses, a few stubby whiskers jutting out from his chin. There was a pause in which he seemed to read the expression on my face and, somehow, understand what I required.

"Someday," he began, still smiling, "someday, Phil, someone will tell you that those are *just* clouds."

I was too young and paranoia-free to consider the whispering voice in my consciousness and my godfather's comment as a statistically improbable coincidence. Besides, his thoughts and my own had often seemed synchronized somehow. I turned to look at him.

"What do you mean?" I asked, still confused.

A wise, wizened smile rippled across his face—one that, in retrospect, seemed the countenance of a wizard.

"Yes, someday people will tell you that those are just clouds, just clouds. But, Phil . . . don't you believe it," he said with all the assertive conviction that a truly gentle man can muster.

"Don't you believe it."

Now, decades later, I am grateful that I don't believe it. That within the clouds, grasses, cracks of lightning, snowdrifts, and sparkling stars, I am blessed to perceive a mysterious yet evolving spiritual presence that is far more than a "just" or a "mere" or a "simply." I hope you are so blessed as well.

This book is a small affirmation of this mystery, one that is shared by many, some consciously and others only in some vague or unrecognized sense. It is about the presence of the sacred within that which so many now perceive as the secular, the ordinary, and the mundane. It is about how to find confluence and connection with this presence and, in doing so, to discover a clearer sense of direction, purpose, and identity in one's life.

It is about nature's ways.

CHAPTER 1

The Way

To the dull mind nature is leaden. To the illumined mind the whole world burns and sparkles with light.
—Emerson

If one way be better than another, that you may be sure is nature's way.
—Aristotle

This book is for nature mystics, both those who have experienced this state of being and those who aspire to do so.

Don't let the word "mystic" scare you off. Most of us have enjoyed interludes of nature mysticism without ever labeling them as such. Certainly, this kind of consciousness is common among the very young. Watch enough kids in the outdoors and you'll see it on their faces, in their eyes, and spilling from their mouths in expressions of delight and fascination. As Socrates said, "Wisdom begins in wonder." And many an adult enters this existential space as well, whether mesmerized by a stunning sunset or spellbound beneath a night sky exploding with stars.

So if you are someone who longs to loosen the restraints of your ego, soulfully interact with the Creation, and learn the language and wisdom of nature's ways, I welcome you. Whether you are a lifelong devotee of the transcendence the natural world can provide or someone who has only recently awakened to the spiritual depth and sagacity it has to offer, I hope you will find on these pages food for thought . . . but more than that. If the ideas and stories here motivate you to explore the way of the nature mystic, then this tome will have fulfilled its purpose.

And what is a nature mystic? A person who, when in the presence of the natural world, has a full soul. Someone who has been spiritually sculpted by interactions with nature in ways that are enlightening, livening, and transcendent, not to mention just plain wondrous. People who harbor so deep a bond with the Creation that, no matter what befalls them in life, it always provides a sanctuary and a place of worship. Therein, they are as close as they can be to whatever they consider their god.

Despite my lifelong affinity for what most call "the great outdoors," it took me a few decades to realize that this attraction was not simply about good feelings, sensory delights, and wild adventures. For me it has been and remains a deeply spiritual path, one that has constituted my primary faith journey. The day this full realization came to me, I called a dear friend who shares my bond with the natural realm.

"Baggie," I began, "I just realized that you are a nature mystic."

There was a brief pause on the other end, and then he replied, "Is there any other kind?"

What does nature have to do with a mystical state of being?

Well, first off, it is our primal home. As philosopher Alan Watts reminded us, "We don't come into the world; we come out of it." And to it we all return. Deep in our synapses and within the infinitesimally tiny structures of each cell and atom in our bodies, nature is bedrock. It is the whatever-it-is that we call the "life force," an invisible energy that permeates the entire cosmos, from massive galaxy to Homo sapiens to miniscule quark, comprising an incredibly complex system that, in aggregate, functions like an intelligent organism in its own right. Over endless eons of time that stretch beyond our mental horizons and then simply disappear, this force has continuously created and transformed all the structures and processes that constitute our universe.

It's a powerful thing—the most powerful one we know.

And when we go, mind open and with soul, into the natural world, it is this power that we encounter and in which we dwell. It is there, while in the presence of this most elemental and vital of all forces, that we can recognize what is unshakably true in ourselves and in this strange trip called "existence."

There is the social you. There is the self-reflective you. There is the private you. And then, at the core, there is the essential you, the one that remembers in a diffuse way what it was like to be outside of time, unfettered by space, and immersed in a unity beyond all things. Some call it the "oceanic feeling." Others name it "cosmic consciousness" or simply "the all." No matter the labels. Nature can open a door to one's innermost self, to the immutable core of your consciousness that is unencumbered by the world of people, deadlines, egos, and tasks.

Nature's ways. They can be our ways as well, should we choose to travel them. Since the ancients first deified the Sun as the primary source of all life (which, on our planet, is quite literally true), we have understood that there is a power and purpose to the natural world that is far greater than any technology or intelligence possessed by the so-called smart ape, Homo sapiens. Genuine power is not in skyscrapers or missiles or machines. It is in hurricanes, earthquakes, volcanoes, floods, supernovas, quasars, and black holes. It is in the birthing of stars, the tenacity of the life force, the verdant fields, galaxies, comets, and newborns. And while modern folk have largely lost dialogue with this power, it waits for us to open its doors and learn its ways.

This work is about those ways, or paths, and the experiential doors that, once opened through our senses and consciousness, transport us to the ancient but still fully present miracle of existence itself. Therein we can discover a clearer sense of who we are, why we are, and to what we belong. What's more, we enter the presence of the divine mystery—that which sustains our bodies, innervates our consciousness, and infuses our souls.

So I invite you to join me in exploring nature's ways.

They can be your way, our way . . . *the* way.

CHAPTER 2

It's Alive

Every individual is an expression of the whole realm of nature, a unique action of the total universe.

—Alan Watts

A human being is part of a whole, called by us the "Universe," a part limited in time and space. He experiences himself, his thoughts and feelings, as something separate from the rest—a kind of optical delusion of his consciousness. This delusion is a kind of prison for us, restricting us to our personal desires and to affection for a few persons nearest us. Our task must be to free ourselves from this prison by widening our circles of compassion to embrace all living creatures and the whole of nature in its beauty.

—Albert Einstein

How do you feel after you've been face-to-face or skin-to-skin with the natural world?

Whether it was a meander through a park, basking in the summer sun, plunging into a crystal clear lake, getting soaked down by a cold rain, or hauling your rear and forty pounds of gear up some gut-busting trail, I'm betting you felt more alive. It's not always pleasant out there, and if you don't know what you're doing, sometimes it can kill you, but for good or ill, nature is as real as real gets. You feel more alive when you're in contact with the natural world because it *is* alive . . . all of it.

If that's not true for you, if you feel estranged from nature and regard it as a contentious neighbor who must be accommodated or endured, or simply a large, complex, and mindless machine, then you're depriving yourself of a richness found nowhere else in our existence. In a deeply spiritual sense, you are making yourself homeless. After all, we are children of the Earth, as it is of the Sun that, in turn, is of our solar system, which itself is a miniscule part of our galaxy, which is but one of hundreds of billions of galaxies, each with hundreds of billions of stars and countless planets. That's what a tree in the park, a wispy cloud passing overhead, or the robin's call connect us with—an awesome something born of one wondrous and mysterious beginning in the distant past. These connections carry us home, reuniting us from whence we came.

The universe is mind-blowingly vast and intricate, and within it are a near infinity of objects, forces, and events—just a riot of stuff all moving and morphing endlessly. It is a cresting surge of creative possibilities being played out in all manner of forms, happenings, and processes. As author Annie Dillard wrote, "In nature, improbabilities are the one stock in trade. The whole creation is one lunatic fringe. No claims of any and all revelations could be so far-fetched as a single giraffe."

We and all else in the Creation are imbedded in and connected with this unfolding miracle. We are all one. I am not being flowery or metaphorical here. This is quite literally true. Humans are individual manifestations of the force that birthed the entire cosmos. Put another way, we all have the same mother. This elemental energy that emanated from the universe's genesis some 13.7 billion years ago (according to the "big bang" theory) courses through our bodies, the bugs and bacteria, the rivers, the atmosphere, the Oort Cloud (Google it), interstellar space, and everything else we can detect. Not only are you in the universe . . . the universe is in you. The atoms that make up your body and all that you see around you were born in the hearts of stars. As songstress Joni Mitchell sang, "We are stardust." Literally.

Yet this force also transcends the material, doing so through the enigmatic mystery we call "consciousness." Fortunately, we humans have the capacity to use our version of consciousness (there are many others) to seek and experience communion with the Creator, whatever you hold that to be. What's more, there is mounting evidence that what we commonly associate with conscious awareness, such as the capacities to change, communicate, respond to the environment, and evolve, is present in most, if not all entities, things, and processes in nature. So when we connect soulfully with the Creation, we are interacting with far more than material forms, but also with the capacity within such forms to be aware, intelligent, and creative.

So how does one connect with this mysterious whatever-it-is that inhabits all matter and energy?

If you pause now and tune in to your body, you can feel the primal force that gave birth to the cosmos still moving inside of you, in your diffuse body energy, the beating of your heart, your breathing, and so on. The élan vital that enervates you is the same essential whatever-it-is that makes the entire universe alive, not just the forms we have arbitrarily decided are animate or living, like you and birds and lilies, but everything.

Unfortunately, the most common vision we have toward life is narrowed by hubris, by the mindless and scientifically groundless assumption that humans are the sliced bread of Creation and that all else is somehow lesser stuff. In our arrogance, we fail to recognize that all forms, animate and seemingly inanimate, are derived from the same elemental power and are sculpted from a common origin—the birth of time and space that gave rise to existence billions of years ago.

When we examine the stuff of the cosmos at the subatomic level (incredibly tiny), everything appears alive. In fact, energy is what constitutes all forms, from rocks to rhesus monkeys to interstellar nebulae. Physicists tell us that matter is simply energy that has congealed in particulate form. Which means that you and I are energy that has percolated, through the magic of the life force, into what is basically tangible stuff. But magically, even stuff that appears to be solid, like us, is mostly empty space. In fact, most of the cosmos is empty space with little specks of matter scattered about, of which we are a case in point. An atom is 99 percent empty space, and almost all the matter in the cosmos is made of atoms, so this firm-looking world of ours is actually quite spectral.

But here's the paradox, and mysteries have lots of paradoxes, so get used to them. This so-called empty space that claims 99 percent of everything, including you and me, isn't totally empty after all. It just looks empty to us because there isn't any matter occupying it. However, this not-really-empty space is somehow innervated with the four fundamental forces of our universe: Gravity, electromagnetism, the weak nuclear force, and the strong nuclear force. If interested in the details, look them up.

So if you consider something that most humans regard as inert or not alive, such as a stone, lake, or cloud, it helps to remember that, like us, these entities are made up of atoms, which are simply energy in a material guise. Now, atoms move around a lot, coalesce into an infinite variety of shapes, then discombobulate and re-emerge as newer forms, and so on. Nature is a massive recycling system, both at the atomic level (incredibly small) and on a galactic scale (unimaginably massive). So when scientists examine physical reality by peering deep down into the smallest realms of matter (the quantum world), they discover that everything is a moving, morphing sea of energy, meaning that what constitutes a grain of sand is no less alive than what constitutes the cells in your body and, eventually, you. Granted, as atoms come together in different forms and processes, some (like us) become more animate, while others (like sand) become less animate. But at the most basic of levels, we're all made of the same essential stuff, and that stuff is alive.

Rather than regarding some forms or processes as living and others as dead or inert, nature mystics view life as a continuum that encompasses everything in the cosmos—crows, rocks, eagles, water, oxygen—you name it. To them, a stone is alive, but it exists on a far different and less animate part of the life continuum than, say, a fox or a mushroom. So a cloud, for instance, is not a lifeless conglomeration of water vapor, ice, and dust. It is a living form, a vibrant tapestry that is distinctly different than a human, but composed of the same essential whatever-it-is that constitutes everything we perceive as matter or energy.

But however one chooses to slice and dice such ideas, you can feel the afterglow of the cosmos' birthright inside your own sinew and flesh. The calcium in your bones was spewed out into the universe eons ago by exploding stars. So were the elements that make up the rest of your body, not to mention this book. And inside all this stuff is the capacity to evolve and morph into all manner of forms and transformative processes, including hominids like us.

This fundamental energy is in everything. Some of us call it the "life force," while others simply define it as "energy" or, if you're a Star Wars groupie, simply "the force." It really doesn't matter what we call it, unless we just want to argue over who has a better label for something that eludes naming. Granted, you can feel it and it is you and you are crafted from it, but you can't understand this force in a thinking sort of way. It is a truth that must be felt. And that's where the mystical part comes in. Nature's ways must be lived, not just cogitated. There is no power in this book unless it convinces you to open your heart and spirit to the Creator's majesty.

Now, before you decide that I'm certifiable (which is certainly possible), remember that most of what I've asserted here is largely supported by science. Read your quantum physics and cosmology, with a bit of evolutionary biology thrown in, and you'll come across references to pretty much everything I've propounded. And what you'll find there comes from rock-solid egghead people—you know, scientists—many of who end up delving so deeply into the mystery of the Creation that a spiritual door opens to them. They perceive something that is ineffable, that can't be put into words nor understood in concepts. But through their scientific explorations, these people get a glimpse of the genius of the Creator, and many are more or less dumbstruck, amazed, and zapped by the whole thing. Some begin mentally shape-shifting into philosophers, poets, and even mystics. Actress Jodie Foster's character, Dr. Arraway, in the movie *Contact* (from Carl Sagan's novel about an encounter with aliens) said it best when she was transported to other worlds: "They should have sent a poet." It's futile to attempt to cram miracles into literal words or symbols.

As we examine the evidence from science that aligns with a spiritual view toward nature, we discover clear connections between the empirical and the mystical. Consider my assertion that all is one and interconnected. This has been proposed by sages and prophets for thousands of years, but not until fairly recently was there science to back them up.

For example, at the subatomic level (almost too small to imagine) physicists detect a phenomenon they call the "quantum foam," a kind of ocean of energy that gives rise to all the matter and processes in the universe. They speak of us, and all other forms and happenings, as "ripples" within this sea-like foam of energy. And that's what actual ripples are—waves of energy passing through a medium, such as water, air, or tomato soup. This sea of energy we are swimming in is a unified whole, but within this unity we find the ripples, the seemingly infinite expressions of individual things and events, including us. Much of the time most of us feel entirely separate from this unified field of energy. Because we are ripples, so to speak, we have trouble recognizing that we are, at the same time, immersed in the oneness of it all.

To our thinking minds, it seems like a contradiction or paradox, and it is, but only because we don't often feel our connection to this greater unity. When a nature mystic soulfully interacts with the natural world, this seeming paradox is resolved. The light and dark, the tiny and massive, life and death, time and eternity, creation and destruction—all these polarities are in balance within the Creation. And that's where we can go to experience the resolution of confusing opposites and to recognize that our sense of separateness is an illusion. When we interact with nature in a soulful way, we snuggle up to this sense of oneness and connectedness.

OK, so if you've made it this far, you may be wondering, "What's his point?" Well, it's simple really.

Nature is a way into the spiritual, the divine.

By consciously cultivating an I-Thou relationship with the natural world (one based on the communion of two subjects), as opposed to an I-it transaction (an interaction of a subject and a thing), we open a door to experiences that will afford us wisdom, humility, faith, hope, joy, self-knowledge, and the spiritual sculpting of the Creator's hand. It is no accident that virtually all of humankind's greatest prophets, from Jesus to Buddha to Mohammed to Abraham, and countless others, including many women who were not recognized as such, had their souls carved by the spiritual resonance of nature, by the desert and mountaintop and jungle and garden and sea. For many, their spiritual awakenings, or epiphanies, occurred while in communion with the natural world, which constitutes the substantive manifestation of the divinity they sought. When we go to nature with what I call soulfulness (to be examined shortly), we embrace our deepest self as well as the Creation, for we are of it and within it, as it is within us. We are the pup snuggling in its mother's fold, suckling on the spiritual sustenance that we must obtain, lest we perish inside.

So that's my point. And now I'd like to make it more emphatically, not as I just have from a stratospheric intellectual perspective, but as it actually unfolds in the natural world and in the lives of people, on ground level. The remainder of this tome examines how we modern humans can discover and follow nature's ways. It is a path that doesn't always make you feel better, but it definitely makes it possible for you to *be* better. There are many paths to knowing one's self, to obtaining some grasp of what human existence is all about, and to growing a soul, not just an ego. Nature is by no means the only path in this regard, but it differs markedly from many others. It is not so much an inward journey as an outward one, although it leads to the same place. When most of us go looking for our souls, we go "inside" in some fashion. However, through nature, we go outside to find our inside.

This is not doublespeak. Because all are one, when we soulfully touch nature, we touch ourselves, and deeply. By going outward, we journey inward, literally finding ourselves by looking in the place we might least expect.

So what do you say?

Want to take a look?

CHAPTER 3

Soulfulness

Mysticism . . . is the art of establishing conscious relation with the Absolute.

—Evelyn Underhill

If we could see the miracle of a single flower clearly, our whole life would change.

—Buddha

The modus operandi of the nature mystic is soulfulness, which is basically a sensory-based experience that alters one's consciousness by diluting the ego and amplifying one's sense of oneness with the Creation.

I often describe soulfulness as "extroverted meditation." In this regard, it is closely related to "mindfulness," which is a moving meditation characterized by non-attached awareness of one's ongoing experience. Rather than sitting in the traditional lotus posture with eyes closed, focused on one's breathing or on a repetitive mantra, practitioners of mindfulness meditate while going about their daily routines. They do so by focusing their awareness on the here-and-now flow of their experiences. It is an antidote for the frenetic, mindless hyperactivity that pulls so many of us out of the eternal present and into the there-and-then (the absent past and presumed future).

Soulfulness differs from mindfulness by virtue of its focus—nature. It involves escaping the formidable boundaries of the ego, which likes to exist in its own little bubble of self-absorption and presumed importance, in order to experientially join one's psyche and spirit with the natural environment and its myriad manifestations. Soulfulness draws us closer to the sacred consciousness that is incarnate in space, time, matter, and energy. Through it, one discovers that every thing and process in nature is imbued with this mysterious power we call the life force. When in a soulful state, we experience all phenomena as alive and sentient.

Now, there is some anthropological research suggesting that the most frequent catalyst for mystical experiences is nature—first and foremost direct interaction with the natural world and, secondarily, contact with artistic representations of nature, such as paintings, photography, recorded sounds, etc. This is consistent with an earlier assertion by philosopher Aldous Huxley who, in part, proposed that mystical oneness with nature immerses us in the "Divine Ground," which science would regard as synonymous with the quantum foam. Put another way, nature is a doorway to mystical communion with the divine.

Nature affords us many experiential doors that, if opened and followed, reduce or even eliminate our sense of separation and alienation from Huxley's Divine Ground. Most of us have, by happenstance, walked through some of these gateways, only to turn back before journeying more deeply into the experiences they make available. If you have ever been genuinely smitten by a radiant sunset, a rainbow set against a stormy sky, the hiss of snow falling in a dark woods, or the melodic singing of birds, then a door has been presented to you and opened, even if just a crack, affording you an experience of soulfulness. Most of us assume that, as such, these doors simply lead to an encounter with nature's beauty, and we leave it at that. But there is more within. Much more, as many have reminded us.

Meister Eckhart, one of Christianity's greatest mystics, wrote of moments when "all blades of grass, wood, and stone, all things are One." In his meditations involving nature, he entered a sublime awareness that enveloped his ego as the air does your breath on a cold morning. As he wrote, "Apprehend God in all things, for God is in all things. Every single creature is full of God and is a book about God. Every creature is a word of God."

Jean Jacque Rousseau, one of the great philosophers of the Enlightenment, wrote similarly of his evenings on an island lake:

"I liked then to go and sit . . . in some secluded spot by the lake; there the noise of the waves and the movement of the water, taking hold of my senses and driving all other agitation from my soul, would plunge me into delicious reverie in which night often stole upon me unawares."

For him, the spiritual portal presented by nature was sensory absorption in the rhapsody of water, waves, and wind, which is characteristic of soulfulness. Surrendering to it, he was transported into a timeless state of peace and rapture.

Noted anthropologist Joseph Campbell said that God is the experience of looking at a tree and saying, "Ah!" He recognized that any manifestation of nature has the potential to connect with our consciousness and trigger recognition of the spiritual oneness of the Creation, as well as our small but meaningful part within it.

I am reminded of a teaching tale from the Zen Buddhist Master Gensha:

Monk:	"Where can I enter Zen?"
Gensha:	"Can you hear the babbling brook?"
Monk:	"Yes, I can hear it."
Gensha:	"Then enter there."

From the Native American tradition, there are the words of Tatanka Ohitika (Brave Buffalo), a Lakota shaman:

"When I was ten years of age I looked at the land and the rivers, the sky above, and the animals around me and could not fail to realize that they were made by some great power. I was so anxious to understand this power that I questioned the trees and the bushes. It seemed as though the flowers were staring at me, and I wanted to ask them, 'Who made you?'"

How many times have you paused to listen, in the broadest possible sense, to the babbling of a brook, the shush of a waterfall, or the timeless rhythm of waves meeting the shore? Perhaps, in those moments, nature momentarily held you as it whispered to your soul through the "flesh" of the Creation. Maybe, even if briefly, time slowed, your thoughts went mute, you forgot yourself and your life, and there was only that ethereal whisper through the opened door.

For those who wish to enter into the mystery of Creation, who long for relationship with the divine, who want to leave the prison cell of the ego and take spiritual flight, nature provides ways. These are not the paths of some human-made religion or pedantic ritual but, rather, the uncensored expression of the Creator in material form.

Soulfulness, then, is a state of being that creates and sustains a mystical engagement with nature. So let's consider what being soulful requires of us.

Our day-to-day consciousness is often based on the perception and belief that Creation is a multiplicity of individual things. Human consciousness, in particular, experiences itself as a separate entity; in our case, an individual brain with a distinct sense of "me" moving around with the aid of a body. Put another way, most of us experience ourselves somewhat like raindrops, which are distinct caplets of water suspended in the atmosphere and differentiated from everything else by a border. In contrast, during periods of soulfulness, the nature mystic experiences her or himself as immersed in a sea, as part of a continuous, flowing essence that has no boundary, no beginning, and no end. While everyday, rational consciousness is granular and fragmented, mystical awareness is cohesive and boundless. It may be as a close as we get to the experience of eternity, at least in this world.

Another way to envision this mystery is to observe waves. Like us, each wave appears to be an individual entity, one that is distinct from the body of water through which it travels, just as we appear separate from the environment we inhabit. However, as physicists tell us, a wave is not really a mass of moving water particles. In fact, a wave is actually energy that travels through the water and, as it does, the water particles it passes through do not move with it but simply spin in circles. The same is true for a sound wave. Air particles don't travel along with a wave of sound; instead, they simply oscillate back and forth as the energy of the sound vibrates and flows through them. In other words, the water and air are mediums through which energy passes. In kind, to a nature mystic, an individual entity is flowing energy masquerading as a solid, immutable phenomenon, much like a wave.

So when one's consciousness escapes the illusion of being separate from the rest of nature and embraces this holistic reality through direct experience (soulfulness), rather than simply through thought, there is an occurrence of Chinese philosopher Lao Tzu's "primal union"—a sense of oneness with the Creation as a whole.

Soulfulness is the nature mystic's path to this primal union, a path through which her or his senses, consciousness, and spirit become immersed in the natural world. Learning soulfulness is entirely experiential. You have to do it, not just think it. And the first step is usually through one's senses—seeing, hearing, feeling, smelling, etc. As the renegade psychoanalyst Fritz Perls admonished us, "Lose your mind and come to your senses." Very apt advice for the would-be nature mystic.

In the realm of spiritual self-discovery, approaches based on science, philosophy, and rationalism have limited reach. If you wish to truly discover the sacred in nature, you will do well to follow the path of the mystic. At some point, that will require putting this book down, opening the door, and going to meet the Creator.

Now, while some mystics come in very strange and eccentric packages (as do many non-mystics), just as many or more are, by observable standards, quite ordinary. Alan Watts characterized most mystics as follows:

"They are natural and easy in manner; they give themselves no airs; they interest themselves in ordinary everyday matters, and are not forever talking and thinking about religion. For them, there is no difference between spirituality and usual life."

With regard to nature, mysticism is a way of both *being in* the natural world and of *being in relation with* that realm. It is not a personal marketing campaign for telling the rest of the species that one is special.

What the nature mystic senses in the Creation is, quite simply, the sacred, the divine, the transcendent. Everywhere that she or he looks, the Creator looks back. Each time that a nature mystic brings his or her "I" into contact with the natural realm, he or she experiences a "Thou," not an "it." So it is essentially a manner of perceiving, of seeing the beatific in what most regard as the ordinary or simply the pleasing or beautiful. Like the aesthetically sensitive person who can absorb the mesmerizing nuances of a song, painting, or sculpture, the nature mystic "sees" far more than most. To her or him, there is no such thing as "just clouds" or a "mere toad" or "an ordinary tree." As Thomas Jefferson, something of a nature mystic for his time, put it, "There is not a sprig of grass that shoots uninteresting to me."

If you choose to follow the ways of nature, it is this mystical consciousness that will be your vehicle, your ship of passage. So how to begin?

It may be helpful to realize that the spiritual development afforded by following nature's ways, as well as other sacred paths, has a certain "two steps up and one step back" rhythm. The "steps back" that often accompany uplifting and sacred experiences within nature, while not always welcome, are an important aspect of the overall process. Often, they emanate from a wisdom within us that says to that striving part of us, "enough, for now." Like the body, the soul needs its rest.

Overall, there are a few guiding principles to keep in mind while journeying through the ways of nature:

- *Tune your consciousness to nature's ways.* While mindfulness is a proven method for keeping one's awareness focused on the here-and-now, nature mystics employ a variation on this approach, which I call soulfulness. Now, mindfulness suggests that the mind is both the instrument of present-centered awareness and also the recipient of it (as in "filling" the mind with input from the here-and-now). However, to the nature mystic, consciousness is not confined to the brain or mind, but is an elemental attribute of one's entire being (and all of Creation). So what we seek to "fill" by paying attention is our essential self—the soul—not just the mind. Soulfulness, then, is an act of trust in the moment, a way to ride the crest of the universe's surging waves of creative becoming. Now, in learning soulfulness, your thinking mind will likely intrude in an effort to lure your consciousness away from the present. The most effective antidote for this is sensory absorption—"thinking" through your sense organs rather than through your prefrontal cortex. By focusing your awareness on sights, sounds, smells, touches, and (careful now) tastes in the natural world, you can keep the intellect's chatter to a minimum. Through this manner of attending, you will begin to experience the Creation as a Thou, rather than an "it," and your soul will be filled.

- *Be found.* Many of us suffer from a condition I call "control madness," which is basically the compulsion to manage and regulate one's experiences according to some preconceived experiential blueprint. However, the natural world is more about flow and balance than it is about rigid control and planned management, so if you approach nature interaction with a set of burdensome expectations based on what you believe should happen (think ego), soulfulness will be out of reach. As you work your way through this book, you will read many references to "being found" by something in nature. This refers to an important aspect of soulfulness, which is based more on surrendering to one's interactions with the Creation rather than trying to manage them. Instead of going out to *find* a particular experience in the natural world, the nature mystic opens her or himself to being *found by* meaningful experiences that nature provides. Soulfulness, then, involves opening one's self to what nature has to offer and teach, while keeping the ego's expectations in check. If this sounds a bit fuzzy, bear with me. It will become clearer in succeeding chapters.

- *Surrender.* With personal safety always at the top of the list, within your safe zone in nature, let it guide you. If it draws you in to focus (use soulfulness) on some object, entity, or process, and there is no discernible danger in doing so, follow its lead. Be open to what nature's ways may present to you spontaneously (to being found), because once you create an I-Thou rapport with the Creation, it will not only speak to you but also instruct you. Remember, you are not interacting with an unconscious organic machine out there. This is an I-Thou liaison between entities that are both manifestations of the creative energy that birthed and sustains the cosmos.

- *Show reverence.* Nature is sacred. Consider ways to act accordingly in its presence. This can be done in both one's pragmatic existence (minimizing your environmental imprint) and in one's spiritual life. For some, this finds expression as praying, performing ceremonial rituals or employing songs, chants, drumming, or other celebrations of the Creation. Basically, incorporate whatever rituals or means of expression you believe will enliven your spiritual posture toward the natural world. Some of the methods described in succeeding chapters will provide examples in this regard. The purpose of genuine reverence is the expression of love. Nature mystics grow to deeply love and worship the Creation.

With these navigational aids in mind, what follows are descriptions of a few methods for finding the spiritual channels afforded by the natural realm. Each "way" provides a sort of door that leads to what the mystic seeks—the sacred implicit within the Creation. At times, we must simply approach these mystic portals and wait, revisiting them in the hope that an opening will occur. While this seemingly passive modality may not appeal to folks who are disciplined taskmasters, often it seems to be what is required. You may get to run the logistics of your life through management, effort, and force of will, but you don't get to run the cosmos.

So now, let's look at a few paths that nature mystics pursue to find confluence with the Creation. Together, let us walk some of nature's ways.

Chapter 4

Doors

As you sit on the hillside, or lie prone under the trees of the forest, or sprawl wet-legged by a mountain stream, the great door that does not look like a door opens.

—Stephen Graham

Those who soulfully immerse themselves in the natural world are likely, at some juncture, to encounter one of the "doors" I have previously referenced. Essentially, these are experiential pathways that, if entered, can create a mystical or spiritual awareness of the Creation. By pursuing any of the "ways" that we will shortly examine, one can increase the probability that one of these perceptual doorways will appear.

Jonathan, a forty-something aspiring nature mystic who made his living as a lawyer, was a case in point. Having sought my guidance in learning and applying soulfulness, he was persistent in seeking the sacred in the natural world. An avid hiker, frequent kayaker, and cross country skier, he was no stranger to wild places and had attained a confident comfort in being alone in woods or on water. Since his youth, he had relished time outdoors, but his sense for the sacred in nature had always been more of a whisper, a gentle tugging on his awareness suggesting "There is more." He wanted to know what that "more" was all about.

On the day when he encountered this "more," Jonathan was on one of his many day hikes in a large conservancy area, a foray that started with no indication it would be anything other than a pleasant ten-mile loop through hilly, forested terrain. With several miles behind him, he paused at a nondescript point on an elevated and heavily wooded portion of the trail. What motivated him to stop he could not pinpoint, although he later labeled it as "intuition." People who are experienced in the wild sometimes talk about a sixth sense that emerges as their rapport with nature grows more intimate. It may represent some sort of subliminal perception concocted from a wide array of sensory inputs and fueled by their enhanced sensitivity to the nuances of their surroundings. This attribute is most pronounced in native and indigenous peoples who live within nature rather than apart from it. Their capacity to see, hear, smell, perceive, and simply sense more acutely is legend among those who are deficient in this capacity. Given his years of outdoor experience, Jonathan probably has more of this perceptual attribute than most.

"Although you've tried to cure me of it, I've always been more of a power hiker than a stop-and-smell-the-flowers type, but I just stopped in my tracks. Not sure why. I just had a sense of something off the trail to the right. I saw a deer path, so I followed it down," he explained.

"Down" consisted of a quarter mile descent along a well-worn animal trail into a wetland at the base of an expansive bowl-like opening. It was surrounded on all sides by high timber and thick underbrush. The bowl was perhaps a quarter mile across, had open water in the middle, and was ringed with stands of cattails and spongy marsh grass. It was the kind of area that was tucked away, that one could easily walk by on the adjacent trail and never detect.

"It's real nice down there," Jonathan recalled, "but nothing spectacular. I mean, I've seen a lot of really pretty country over the years, so I'm not easily impressed."

"But something happened that left an impression," I suggested.

"That's for sure," he agreed, shivering involuntarily a bit at the recollection.

Employing what he had learned about soulfulness, Jonathan paused to drink in the vista before him, doing his best to absorb the ambience in his midst. After a few minutes, he suddenly felt an odd change in his sensory perceptions. It began first with his sight.

"This will sound weird, but everything started to get . . . well, to become sort of fuzzy. It was like things weren't solid anymore," he struggled to explain.

Next it was his hearing.

"Then I heard this white noise sound, almost like static on the radio but not so harsh," he continued.

In fact, Jonathan's entire sensory repertoire was gradually being transformed. Smells became more pungent. The sensation of the wind on his skin was exquisitely amplified. The feel of the mushy ground underfoot seemed to migrate up into his legs and torso, as if, to use his words, he was "melting" into the soil. So smitten was Jonathan by this sensory metamorphosis, that he spontaneously adopted one of the most rare mental states for people in our frenetic modern era.

He stopped thinking.

"I studied meditation once for a few months, and it drove me nuts because I just couldn't shut off my mind," he explained. "But when all this was happening, I wasn't thinking a single thought."

However, what most surprised and somewhat unnerved Jonathan was one overriding characteristic of what he beheld and felt.

"It was like nothing was solid anymore. It seemed like everything, including me, was just like light or sparkling energy or something," he said.

It was this portion of the event that served to pop this gentleman's emotional rivets. His thinking mind, as if stunned and staggered by the abruptness and intensity of what had taken place, suddenly came to and howled in fear and protest, demanding to somehow make sense of it all. Nowhere in his library of experiences could he recall anything so bizarre and inexplicable, beautiful and transcendent as it was. There were no points of reference in his memory.

"When I started thinking again, the first thing that came into my mind was to realize how far out the whole experience seemed. I mean, I didn't know what was happening, what to make of it, or even how long I'd been there," he explained.

"How long did that last?" I asked.

"I haven't a clue. As far as time, I was as disoriented as I've ever been in my life."

As Jonathan slowly collected himself intellectually and began to reclaim his orientation regarding time, place, and circumstances, his ego chimed in, not surprisingly, with all manner of paranoia. Struggling to make sense of what, to his intellect, was virgin experiential territory, his ego offered a series of potential explanations.

Was he ill? This didn't seem likely, as he was in excellent health and had been eating and drinking properly throughout his hike.

A seizure? He'd never had one and there was no family history . . . but maybe.

Exhaustion? Stamina had always been his forte, and the demands of the day's hike had been mild by his standards.

The last and, to him, most likely possibility then entered his mind.

"I'm losing it."

Although not sophisticated about psychology, Jonathan knew enough to consider that he might be having an anxiety attack or, for him, some other uncharacteristic mental event. But that notion felt so disconnected from what he had just experienced that it seemed simply implausible. He had coped with anxiety before, particularly in some dicey wilderness situations, and this felt abjectly different.

"So after the paranoia welled up, what did you do?" I asked.

"I sat down," he replied. "Intuitively, I felt that I should get close to the ground, like for a foundation or something. Everything was so confusing. I just needed one thing to be solid."

Sitting there on the soggy, matted soil, his mind racing, his senses crackling with hypersensitivity, Jonathan did what most veteran outdoor-types do when lost (in this case, only metaphorically). Nothing. He took a time out. At one point, he lay flat on his back, opening his arms to the sky and more or less surrendering himself to the flash flood of sensation and emotion in which he was being swept along.

"That's when the intensity started to ease up," he told me. "After I just stopped fighting it."

"How did you manage to not fight it?" I inquired.

"I just realized that this was probably one of those doorway events you and I had talked about, and that I was just reacting to it being so new to me. So I just laid there and, slowly, the intensity of the sensations eased off," he explained.

Not surprisingly, Jonathan wanted to comprehend this happening. He felt the need, as most of us do, to label and conceptualize this experience, to put it in the proper place on his intellectual bookcase.

"How do I get to the bottom of this?" he asked.

I smiled at his choice of words and the resulting metaphor, but resisted the impulse to impress him with his own subconscious insight.

"Well, one way of looking at it is that something found you out there," I suggested.

To the nature mystic, the concept of being found is fundamental. For the most part, the seeker cannot go out and, by force of will or effort, create sought-after states of consciousness or specific psycho-spiritual experiences. She or he cannot call forth the "oceanic feeling" of Lao Tzu by power of intention. Rather, we can seek or support conditions, both internal and external, that allow the spiritual forces present in the natural world to come forth. And of course, as Jonathan's happenstance illustrated, there are also times when one is found by these forces even without seeking . . . at least without consciously seeking.

"Perhaps you were found by something greater than yourself," I suggested.

"What?"

"It would be a mistake for me to attempt to answer that," I replied. "You have been invited into a different realm of awareness, a new reality. It's up to you to find or at least seek the answer to that question."

From my perspective, it seemed likely that Jonathan had experienced a brief but powerful interaction with the underlying mystery and power of the life force. For reasons that may never be entirely clear to him or me, a door was opened to him. But a door to what? This is where words and concepts often prove our undoing. The numinous experiences afforded us by the spiritual forces immanent within nature are truly beyond words or even thinking as we customarily conduct it.

So what did Jonathan truly experience? Did he lose the separation between raindrop (individual) and sea (unity) and undergo a transitory state of oneness with the Creation? Did he leave the Newtonian plane of existence and stick a perceptual toe into the sea of the quantum energy that many physicists believe is the élan vital of the cosmos and everything in it? Did he fall, ever so briefly, into the stunning embrace of the Creator and look upon a divine countenance implicit in the natural world?

"If you really want to know, you may want to consider one particular course of action," I suggested.

He looked me long in the eyes.

"You want me to go back there," he concluded.

"Well, there will be no going back to that exact experience because all experiences are unique," I suggested. "But you can go sit by the door again, so to speak."

"And then?" he wondered.

"And then wait to see if it opens. It may. It may not."

So Jonathan returned to the wetland bowl. And predictably, there was no déjà vu, no replication of the unique moments that consumed his consciousness that particular day. His body did not melt into the soil. His thoughts were not struck dumb in their circuitous tracks. The landscape failed to liquefy into a ghostly soup of light and energy.

The so-called same path is never the same. The presumed same place is always different.

"So what was there?" I asked him later.

"The door was there," he answered. "It didn't open again, but I could sense it. The door was there."

And that is, above all else, the sign of one who recognizes that nature is spirit, that, to borrow a Christian metaphor, it is indeed the "Word made flesh." For such a soul, the natural world is a gateway, sometimes closed, other times slightly open and, occasionally, widely beckoning. But even when shut, one can still perceive, albeit in a murky fashion, what resides on the other side.

The Creation had spoken to Jonathan.

For him, "flesh" would never be the same.

CHAPTER 5

The Way of Place

How can you buy or sell the sky, the warmth of the land? The idea is strange to us. If we do not own the freshness of the air and the sparkle of the water, how can you buy them? Every part of the Earth is sacred to my people.

—Chief Seattle

When I pass from this life, I hope my ashes will be scattered in the waters of a small, placid body of water in northeast Illinois where I grew up.

Of the many places I have been blessed to feel an affinity for on this wondrous planet, this, above all others, is my spiritual home. It is the sacred location where my soul feels an unbroken umbilical to the Creation. To me, the water of this little and, to most casual observers, unremarkable lake is holy. Whenever I visit there, I kneel at the shore and anoint myself with it, as a devotee would the holy water from a church or consecrated spring.

While perhaps odd or quaint to some, ceremonial acts of reverence for nature are part of soulfulness. Underpinning such rituals is the idea of place, the sustaining role of geographic locations, natural processes, and objects in creating a sense for and remembrance of the divinity of the natural world.

Many indigenous peoples recognized the role of sacred places in growing their bonds and dialogue with the Creator. For some this involved sensing the spiritual forces and entities inhabiting particular locales, such as mountains, wooded glens, or at the shores of great bodies of water. Often, these numinous environs became sites for conducting religious ceremonies, for solitary contemplation, or vision quests. Like some of the mosques, synagogues, temples, and cathedrals of more recent religious traditions, these hallowed spots in nature were often used for many generations and came to represent vital elements in the spiritual life of tribal peoples. They were, therefore, regarded as sacred and worthy of the utmost respect.

In contrast, today most religious practices are conducted indoors within buildings specifically designed for such purposes. This reflects a near complete reversal of the mindset of early humans. For most modern folk, veneration of the Almighty is largely confined to a temple, church, or mosque, reinforcing the perception that God is separate from the Creation. Whereas a "temple" of towering pines is a direct manifestation of the Creator, one of wood, stone, and marble, while often beautiful and glorious in its own right, is a human representation for or symbol of the divine. Meaning that nature mystics feel a greater connection with the Creator when fully absorbed in its abiding presence in the natural world itself, not while sequestered inside a building. To me, the Creator made its own temple, which we euphemistically refer to as "the great outdoors."

This also translates into collective attitudes toward the natural realm from an environmental standpoint. Once nature has been stripped of its divinity, once God, whatever you hold that to be, resides in a church rather than a mountain stream, oak savannah, or undulating prairie, the admonition to treat the biosphere as a sacred place worthy of respect and protection rapidly diminishes, or disappears altogether. Hence our willingness to defile the sacred sites of indigenous peoples in deference to "economic development," which is too often a euphemism for environmental destruction.

In his book *The Dream of the Earth*, author Thomas Berry recounts a public discussion in 1975 in the Cathedral of the Divine in New York City. One of the principle participants was Lame Deer, a member of the Lakota nation in North America. Berry wrote:

> he [Lame Deer] turned to the audience and remarked on how overpowering a setting [the cathedral] it was for communication with divine reality. Then he added that his own people had a different setting for communion with the Great Spirit, a setting out under the open sky, with the mountains in the distance and winds blowing through the trees, with the earth under their feet, surrounded by the living sounds of the birds and insects. It is a different setting, he said, a different experience, but one so profound that he doubted that his people would ever feel entirely themselves or would ever be able to experience the divine adequately in any other setting.

And so it is with those who embrace the natural world as divine. Even among people who do not, one often hears the remark that they feel "closer to

God" while in a beautiful natural setting than while in a house of worship. In my own experience as a child, raised as I was in the Roman Catholic faith, I soon learned to simply get through mass and other religious ceremonies in our small church and reserve my spiritual reverie and communion for those times when that lake and I were in dialogue.

Can people find resonance with the divine in a holy building? Of course, as they can in a hymn, chant, a painting, sculpture, or any of the other numerous representations of the spiritual. Clearly, a church, shrine, mosque, or temple can assume a kind of spiritual aura, perhaps a cumulative presence created by all the devotees who have worshipped there. So nature mystics do not hold an exclusive claim to the existential doors that await those souls seeking transcendence. Yet they follow pathways that are too often ignored in our world of made-up things.

But just how did it happen that earlier cultures came to anoint a particular place as sacred? Who made this determination, and why? Definite answers are shrouded in the unwritten and increasingly forgotten early history of our species. Nonetheless, we can make some educated guesses.

For one, we know that shamans, the earliest priests of tribal societies, served as intermediaries between the secular and spiritual realms. Unlike many of their modern contemporaries, such as ministers and imams and rabbis, these holy persons were chosen by experience, not by vocational preference or academic training. They underwent transformative events, usually mystical in nature, which demonstrated to them and their communities that they had been selected for this role. As is true today, it is likely that some of them were charlatans. However, those who were the genuine article were purportedly "chosen" by the spiritual forces with which they would later commune in a more ritualized and ceremonial fashion.

It is possible that the physical locations where these "being chosen" experiences occurred were subsequently designated as sites of spiritual power. A more modern representation of this proclivity is found at Lourdes in southern France where millions have come in search of healing. For those unfamiliar with this phenomenon, in 1858 a young peasant girl named Bernadette Soubirous reportedly was visited numerous times in a small grotto by a vision of Mary, the mother of Jesus Christ. According to Bernadette, she was instructed by this vision to build a chapel on the site and to drink from a fountain there. No fountain was evident, but when Bernadette dug at a spot designated by the vision of Mary, a spring began to flow. Many who visit Lourdes and drink from the fountain declare they have been healed, although the Catholic Church only recognizes a handful of these claims as legitimate. So even today we continue to associate place with spiritual power, and these associations are largely based on someone's immersion in a mystical experience either brought about by or associated with the location in question.

Now, the skeptical can certainly assert that what we have here is a correlation, not a cause and effect. Just because two happenings occur at the same time or in close proximity does not mean that one precipitated the other. Because a shaman of some tribe or a saint of some religion fell into a spiritual reverie at a particular location does not mean those physical environs had anything causative to do with her or his transcendent experience. Being at Lourdes and drinking from the fountain may have no spiritual power independent of the hopeful expectation of the pilgrim (the so-called placebo effect). This is the sort of debate that is a matter of faith, not fact, so we shall not settle it here, or elsewhere I suspect.

Nonetheless, from the viewpoint of a nature mystic, some places and natural processes speak to us and, on occasion, serve as doorways to the divine. Sacred locales seem to be so for certain people and not others. Most of those who interact with the lake of my childhood, for example, probably do not regard it as an expression of the sacrosanct, a site of worship, as I do. Because the experience of a sacred place can be idiosyncratic (particular to one individual and not others), there is an implied connection between the "touched" person and the spiritual force immanent in that location or in the natural process itself.

In serving as a spiritual guide for others, I have often encouraged people who cannot already identify a sacred place in their lives to go discover one. As noted previously, this most often is a process of *being found* rather than of finding. While the seeker actively places her or himself in natural environments that may afford a sacred connection or the opening of a spiritual passageway, she or he does not consciously choose precisely where this occurs. Rather, that person is "chosen by" the location and the spiritual energy being manifested there.

It is important to recognize that sometimes a sacred place is actually a sacred process rather than a location. One woman I worked with spent many long treks in nature hoping to be spiritually found by a particular spot, only to return to me in frustration.

"If there is a place out there for me, I haven't found it . . . or it hasn't found me," she reported.

It brought to mind the story of the man who is walking down the street late one night and notices another on his hands and knees, searching among the cobblestones.

"What are you looking for?" he asks.

"I lost my ring," the other fellow replies.

Being a kind soul, the gentleman joins the stranger in his search. After considerable looking without success, he asks, "Are you sure you lost your ring here?"

"Oh no, not here," the man answers. "I lost it over there in the alley."

"Well, then, why are we looking here?" he asks, incredulous.

"Because the light is much better here," the stranger replies.

Translating this into the realm of consciousness, we tend to approach our spiritual quests based on what we already know and can see, rather than opening our awareness to what might be hidden or more difficult to perceive.

So I accompanied this woman on another hike into an old growth forest. We stopped often to simply be conscious of our surroundings and, almost each time, I noticed she was drawn to anything associated with water. She would touch the dewdrops on the leaves, stick her fingers or toes into streams and, later, when it began raining, she made no effort to shield her face. At one point she stopped on the trail, lifted her gaze skyward and met the falling rain, a soft smile on her face.

Turning to me after a bit and noticing my stare she asked, "What is it?"

"You look like someone being found," I replied.

"I feel that way," she answered, a luminosity in her countenance. "You think it's this place?"

"No, I don't," I answered but offered nothing more.

Momentarily confused, she raised her hands and gently caressed the gathering moisture on her face, spreading it over her skin. Lowering her hands, she looked at the water on her palms, glistening. And then one of those "Aha!" smiles erupted on her face.

"It's the water," she whispered, turning to me.

"I believe you," I replied.

"Water is my place," she concluded.

For some I have been honored to guide, their "place" has been the wind, clouds, sunsets, rainbows, star-filled skies, the ancient sound of crickets, snow, butterflies, and other processes or manifestations not tied to a particular location. Nature is not obedient to our taxonomy or penchant for order.

Once recognized, a sacred place or process affords the chosen person a context through which the divinity of nature may be experienced, as well as a sanctuary for personal reflection and emotional healing during times of duress. For the nature mystic, it provides a context for creating symbols, constructing rituals, and performing ceremonies. Minimally, it offers a place or process that is ideal for contemplating the Creation, as well as for pursuing more intensive forms of I-Thou interaction with the natural world, such as through soulfulness.

Paradoxically, being found by a sacred place often requires first becoming lost. Wandering aimlessly in the natural world (first, be sure you know the basics about safety for that particular environment) is frequently a prerequisite for connecting with a place or process. Many of my clients have suffered my admonition to "Go get lost so you can be found."

Once one has been found by a sacred place or process, there is never again a sense in which one feels existentially lost. An umbilical has been grown between one's individual soul and the universal One.

Henceforth, you are forever found.

Method

The Way of Place involves the following:

- A certain amount of wandering in a variety of natural environments.
- While in these locales, opening one's self (soulfulness helps) to receiving what the Creation has to offer. This may arrive as an absorbing fascination with some thing or process, as an inner feeling of awe, reverie, or childlike joy, or a state of consciousness characterized by "Ah!"
- Once found by a place or process, pause to give thanks. And each time you return, consider spending a few moments expressing your gratitude.
- Your sacred place can be employed for a variety of spiritual pursuits, such as soulfulness, inner meditation, rituals, and ceremonies. While there, your activities in this regard will likely be infused with greater spiritual energy, and you may find yourself approaching or experiencing transcendent states of consciousness.
- In addition to its spiritual attributes, a sacred place also provides a refuge during life's emotional or interpersonal storms. Many of my psychotherapy clients are encouraged to visit their sacred locales when they need to make important life decisions, clear their thoughts, de-stress, or promote the healing of emotional wounds. It's good therapy.
- Be aware that, for some, sacred places or processes change over time. If yours begins to lose its power to connect you with the Creation, then you may be receiving an important message—that it's time to move on and be found by another. The path of the nature mystic is a journey, not a destination.

Application

The Way of Place sits well in these circumstances:

- You are spiritually lost, ungrounded, and adrift.

- You feel disconnected from human-made places of worship and desire a new "temple" in which to commune with the divine.
- You have reached the point in your spiritual work where you desire greater outward expression of the I-Thou relationship with the Creation. The Way of Place is well suited to ritual, ceremony, prayer, and worship.
- You feel emotionally wounded or conflicted, and in need of shelter from life's storms.

CHAPTER 6

A Place of Healing

I've always regarded nature as the clothing of God.
—Alan Hovhaness

Keep close to nature's heart, and break clear away, once in a while, and climb a mountain or spend a week in the woods. Wash your spirit clean.
—John Muir

Judith had entered the dark night of her soul. An individual of abounding faith, compassion, and deep reverence for the divine in all people, she found herself becoming lifeless inside, where it counts.

"Looking back, I can see it was gradual," she confided in me. "Sort of like how a flower fades and then dries up. Then it just crumbles and blows away."

Judith's stark, uncompromising description expressed the erosion of spiritual faith that she suffered over the course of several difficult years. As one might expect, this period had pummeled her with a series of taxing losses, from the sudden death of her best friend to serious personal health problems and, as if fate were without mercy, to the end of her 20-plus-year marriage. Each loss compelled Judith to return to the wellspring of her faith, where she sought to dip her heart and soul in its healing waters. However, with slow but inexorable certainty, the well went dry.

"I remember the last time I went to church. I had always felt the presence of God there, but that last time ... well, I might as well have been in Walmart," she concluded.

Judith was not one to jump to conclusions. She gave herself what seemed wise counsel and decided to wait. Perhaps, she reasoned, the abiding sense of the spiritual that had been the core of her existence would return somehow, given enough time, patience, and emotional healing. So she did what she felt might give it a hand. She took care of her health, meditated, sought the company of friends, indulged in music, art, and good books, tried to laugh . . . all the prescriptions for self-healing that experts promote. And of course, she prayed.

"In a lot of ways, I did heal. My body got stronger and my life seemed to settle into a routine and balance out . . . except for one thing," she told me.

That "one thing" was her feeling of spiritual faith, the vital sense of a living bond with a power greater than herself. No amount of re-balancing in her lifestyle or waiting or hoping seemed to make any difference in that regard. The well remained dry. The flower did not rise nor bloom once again.

And so Judith sought my counsel. Hearing of my work with nature therapy and hoping for some salvation through its ministrations, she brought me her story and her poverty of spirit.

"I've never been much of a nature person," she confessed. "Oh, I do love the flowers and birds and mountains . . . all of it . . . but I'm kind of a fair weather naturalist, if you know what I mean."

Judith's idea of connecting with nature consisted of sitting on a porch on a warm, sunny day and gazing out at the greenery and blue skies. At most, she might walk through her neighborhood or a nearby park, enjoying the fresh air and the fragrant flowers. For her, swimming was to be done in pools and gardening always required gloves. Contact with rain, snow, mud, and the other "messy" aspects of the natural environment was to be minimized.

"I guess I'm a city girl," she surmised.

I agreed to work with Judith; however, I warned her that doing so would require a bit more direct contact with the Creation on her part. I pledged to guide her as she discovered this new and, for her, rather foreign relationship, but also insisted that, at some juncture, she and the Creation would have to meet directly, without any intermediary. She agreed, although I suspect more out of desperation than desire.

For a setting, I suggested a large tract of national forest. It was February in Michigan's Upper Peninsula, and while the winter had been cold, there was little snow. Bundled up against the frigid air, we set out on an established hiking trail under a cold but sunny sky. We wound through some older growths of pine on craggy hills, then down to lower glens populated with cedar and some birch. Eventually, the trail opened into a broad wetland riddled with frozen streams and stands of cattails and reeds. The wind had picked up and we began to feel its chill at our backs.

I waited for that perception of place that has become, gratefully, an addition to my usual compliment of senses. If I succeed in relinquishing my thoughts and tune in to the natural environment, sometimes I am blessed to have an intuitive awareness of being in a sacred location, a physical place where the presence of the Spirit seems uncommonly strong, where a "door" is cracked open. This came to me at a creek crossing in a small grove of trees.

"What is it?" Judith asked as I stopped and grew still.

"This may be a doorway," I replied. "Let's be present for a moment and just pay attention."

Judith closed her eyes, lifting her head slightly. She stayed within herself, silently for a time, and then looked at me.

"I don't really feel anything, except maybe really cold," she told me. "I don't feel God's presence inside of me."

"We are not here to find God inside of you," I suggested. "We are here to find God outside of you . . . out there."

Judith looked a bit confused for a moment, and then smiled slightly.

"I hadn't thought of it that way. How do I do that?" she asked.

"Let's find out," I replied. "I doubt I can teach you that, but I suspect that nature can."

I led her along the side of the creek, following an animal trail with fairly fresh deer tracks. It was difficult but not dangerous going, and after about a hundred yards, we drew next to an iced-over wetland marked by a large field of cattails, many well over six feet high.

"Now what?" she asked, her face wrinkled with confusion.

"Now open your senses," I requested. "Mute your thinking mind and just drink in your surroundings. Use your eyes, ears, nose, fingers . . . your senses."

Judith hesitated, then looked around slowly. Cautiously, she stepped down onto the edge of the frozen creek. A thin layer of snow covered the ice, and although the creek was shallow and there were no visible signs of seeping water or weakness, I stayed near just in case. She took a couple of steps, remaining close to the shore. Suddenly a loud crack echoed up from the ice under her feet. Spooked, she leapt up on the shore, then let out a little whoop and laughed at being startled.

"Not that way," she mumbled to herself, turning toward the field of cattails.

She took a few steps out into them, teetering a bit as she strained to master the lumpy terrain of the frozen wetland. Then she stopped, her hands dropping to her sides, as if suddenly aware of something that no one else could perceive.

That was when she first heard the whisper of the Creator.

"It was in the cattails and reeds. I had my back to the wind, the sun was in my face, and I started to hear them . . . I mean *really* hear them," she later explained.

I had heard them as well. The wind was robust and gusty, and it played the brown, supple stalks of the cattails like a chorus of instruments. The sound cascaded across the field in waves, rising crescendos closely followed by waning lulls, then rising once more. The cacophony of "music" was stunning in its variety and subtle beauty. Standing there with her, I had closed my eyes, the brightness of the winter sun still illuminating my inward field of vision, and allowed the symphony of wind and movement to lift my soul, to take me fully in its embrace.

Based on her later account, Judith had felt much the same.

Opening my eyes and looking at her from a few yards away, I saw her face gradually lifting toward the sun, a widening smile sculpting her demeanor. Slowly Judith's arms rose from her sides, rising skyward. She remained that way for a time and then her face changed. The smile persisted but her eyes and forehead crumpled a bit. A big tear rolled down one cheek, then another. Judith's arms lowered and her knees slowly bent until she was kneeling in the snow. Her head came down and her shoulders began to quake. Faint sobs mingled with the windblown cattails, like a new instrument joining the symphonic performance.

God was back in her life.

"I can't explain it," she said later.

"Don't try," I recommended.

Indeed, what Judith felt and heard that February afternoon cannot be captured in language. The best we can do is to represent these kinds of experiences in poetry, music, or art, realizing that even symbolic and expressive mediums fail to convey the ineffable essence of the spiritual energy incarnate in the natural world.

The kind of epiphany that Judith experienced is not so rare as we might imagine. The spiritual is ever-present and available within the material, and it is only our preoccupations with the hard-and-fast elements of life, our propensity for intellectual "aboutism" (thinking *about* something rather than *being with* something), or our inability to tune our consciousness to the unity of things that keeps it invisible. If most of us had been in that field of cattails with Judith that afternoon, and she had turned to us in her bliss and exclaimed, "Can you hear it!" or "Do you feel it?" the majority response might well have been no. Oh, most of us would have heard the wind playing the reeds, but that hearing would likely have been of a very different sort than hers.

Forgive me if I sell too many of us short. There is hearing, and then there is *hearing*. Which is to say that, recording sound with one's ears and synapses is not entirely the same as either experiencing that sound deeply in one's consciousness, or actually soulfully blending with and becoming that sound throughout one's entire being. Most of us can relate to losing ourselves in a wondrous piece of music. Well, nature is an ongoing symphony of sound, and no two "notes" are ever entirely the same.

Judith not only heard the voice of God in the Creation (although that alone is a blessing indeed), she also became that voice, resonating to its harmonies with her innermost being. Like the raindrop, once separate and alone, falling into the sea, she rejoined that which is the source of her individual existence.

Why did this experience come to Judith that day? What factors contributed to its development? If these factors were brought to bear once again, could this epiphany of hers be repeated?

The intellectual nets of our minds strive to capture and control that which we so deeply desire. But we will fail in this. So far as we can discern, the Creation does not repeat itself. While there are similarities, there are not exact replicas. Judith's transcendent moment was unique, a once-in-a-universe happening, a ripple on the vast ocean of existence. It will not submit to our longing to repeat or control it, however well motivated.

"Don't go looking for the same experience," I cautioned her. "In nature, there are no reruns."

"What should I look for?" she asked.

"Place yourself in the relationship, in the presence of the Creator. Stand in the doorways that appear to you, and then ask for and open yourself to what will be given," I suggested.

And when we do, we discover one of the most benevolent and comforting truths of all. We learn, as poet Walt Whitman reminded us, that when all else in this life seems to abandon us—success, pleasure, family, security, passion, health, friends, meaning—nature remains.

The spirit was made material, but it did not cease to be spirit.

And it does not cease to be there for us . . . ever.

CHAPTER 7

The Way of Trees

We can speak without voice to the trees and the clouds and the waves of the sea. Without words they respond through the rustling of leaves and the moving of clouds and the murmuring of the sea.

—Paul Tillich

Many nature mystics are drawn to trees. Gautama Buddha, legend claims, meditated and found enlightenment under a pipal tree (later named the Bodhi Tree). Inversely, the Book of Genesis in the Bible tells how Adam and Eve ate fruit from the tree of knowledge and were subsequently cast out of Eden, which may be a metaphor for oceanic consciousness (feeling at one with the Creation). In fact, many religious texts, psalms, and stories incorporate references to these magnificent entities.

Trees first appeared on Earth about 370 million years ago. It is estimated that there are about 100,000 species comprising roughly 400 billion individual trees that cover about one-third of our planet's landed surface. In the realm of trees, however, the term "individual" can sometimes be misleading. For instance, cyprus and aspen groves, which look like large expanses of separate trees, are sometimes composed of a single connected individual, one that encompasses hundreds of acres.

Canada's boreal forest is the largest contiguous expanse of trees on Earth, covering over 35 percent of that nation's landmass. It demonstrates the vital importance of trees in creating and sustaining different ecosystems and species. For example, Canada's forest is home to the world's largest caribou herd, the second-highest population of wolves, and large groups of polar, black, and grizzly bears, not to mention three billion birds that nest there each year. It is also a major source for regenerating oxygen in our atmosphere, as are all great forests.

The largest tree species is the Giant Sequoia, which can exceed 300 feet in height, over 50 feet in diameter, with a trunk whose weight can eclipse 1400 tons. They start from a seed no bigger than a grain of wheat and can live up to 3500 years. The tallest trees, however, are the redwoods (also part of the Sequoia family), which can top 370 feet. The smallest tree (there is some debate about this) is the pygmy pine, which is native to the alpine regions of New Zealand. Fully grown, this tiny conifer is no larger than a small, short shrub.

Given their age, diversity, and critical role in sustaining other life forms, our bond with trees goes way back.

Our hominid ancestors lived in trees, which were sources of protection, food, mobility, and play, encompassing the neighborhoods that supported the earliest of our tribal families. Without them, there is the possibility that we wouldn't be here. For example, consider the baobab tree found in Africa, where our species had its beginnings. Our ancestors learned to hollow out this tree's huge trunk (50 feet or more in diameter) both for storing water and as living quarters. They ate its leaves, fruit, seeds, and roots, and some people still do. Once our forebears became bipedal, they gradually stopped making their homes in trees and ventured onto the savannahs and plains. But ingrained in our genetic lineage is the primordial memory of this attachment.

The long mutual history may explain why older trees, in particular, seem to draw us to them. Perhaps, in part, we are in awe of creatures that have attained the balance, harmony, and wisdom necessary to survive on the planet far longer than we. Certain species of trees are, in fact, among the most ancient organic entities, as well as the largest of all plants. In this regard, it may be enlightening to consider one in particular.

One of the oldest known living organisms is a 26-foot-high bristlecone pine to which humans have assigned the name "Methuselah." It lives in the desert outside of Las Vegas. Scientists place its age at over 4600 years, meaning it was a seedling when the ancient Egyptians were building their pyramids. When Jesus Christ was born, it had already witnessed the passing of over two millennia.

Bristlecone pines are super tough creatures, living high in the arid White Mountains of California in exceedingly harsh conditions with little water and sparse nutrients. The air is thin, the wind unceasing, and the summer a brief respite of a few lukewarm weeks. Which may explain why the outside of Methuselah is a thick, inert mantle of dense, fibrous bark, while the protected interior is a relatively narrow core that feeds nutrients and moisture up its trunk, sustaining its prolonged existence.

The greatest threat to Methuselah's survival is, not surprisingly, us. It may have come close to dying, as did many of its brethren bristlecones, when miners inundated the area in the 1870s in pursuit of silver. Harvesting the trees to fire their smelting furnaces, they denuded entire mountains. Perhaps one of Methuselah's elders, who today would be older still, fell before the saws and axes of these ecologically unconscious people.

Methuselah lives in one of the driest environments on Earth. Only during the snowmelt of the spring does it drink, taking in about 100 gallons a year. Its needles are designed to preserve moisture, making long and efficient use of an amount that would spell certain doom for any Homo sapiens. In nearby Las Vegas, the average person uses 300 gallons of water per day.

Which creature do you imagine will successfully meet the long-term challenge of survival in an arid ecosystem?

Despite its advanced age there is no indication that Methuselah is dying on its own accord. It continues to reproduce and is still growing every year. Although roughly five millennia old, not long ago it generated a pinecone from which seeds were extracted and germinated at a rate approaching 100 percent. Scientists simply don't know how long it will live.

An even older tree than Methuselah was, inexplicably, cut down. It's well-meaning but ignorant assassin, seeking to study bristlecones, didn't know how to properly extract a core from that tree and so, sadly, felled it with a chain saw in order to obtain a full ring sample. Duh. As if to amplify this cruel fate, part of this ancient tree is now on display in a casino in Las Vegas. It has become a decorative item gazed upon by thousands of souls who likely regard it as a curiosity but little else. But there is a far different and better way to interact with these stunning and ancient life forms.

Creating an I-Thou interaction with a tree comes more naturally to many of us than with, say, the wind or clouds or rocks. Perhaps trees seem more like us, individual entities with unique variations implying personality. This is certainly true of Methuselah. Philosopher Martin Buber, who promulgated the concept of the I-Thou relationship (or what some refer to as subject-to-subject interaction), wrote about his connection with trees in this regard:

> I contemplate a tree . . . I can feel it as movement; the flowing veins around the sturdy, striving core, the sucking of the roots, the breathing of the leaves, the infinite commerce with earth and air . . .

When I behold a tree, I see an entity that is wondrously interwoven with its surrounding environment. It reaches into the breezy ocean of the atmosphere, grasping it with countless branches, stems, leaves, and flowers—a vast network of tributaries suckling the moisture in the air, the carbon dioxide, and the sunlight. The same occurs beneath the surface where a tree's roots engage in a similar symbiosis with water, soil, nutrients, and minerals. It is a superbly adapted creature so intimately in dialogue with its surroundings that the two are quite literally inseparable. The same is true for us, but we rarely feel or act that way.

Now, science confirms that trees do, indeed, exhibit unique variations in their development, suggesting that each is a differentiated entity that possesses both agency and will (like us). For example, a sought-after holy grail of commercial forestry has been the ability to reduce or eliminate variations in tree growth so that a group of seedlings can be managed to produce a highly uniform crop of adult trees. However, this cornfield approach to tree production (as totalitarian states have discovered about managing people) has been subverted by the capacity of individual trees to be just that . . . individuals. So trees of the same species growing in identical soil, climate, and spacing conditions respond uniquely, not uniformly. This implies that trees possess an attribute that cannot be entirely controlled by manipulating environmental conditions (sound familiar?). Each one has a nature or temperament, much like people, that while influenced by the environment, is not wholly controlled by it. The result is extensive variability among individual trees nurtured in near identical conditions.

All of which suggests that trees, like people, are subjects (Thou), not objects (it). And perhaps part of what makes them unique, like us, is their capacity for consciousness, agency, and will—meaning they are aware, actively participating with their environment, and making decisions about how to act and respond. We know, for example, that trees communicate with each other, as well as other entities, such as certain insects. They do so by emitting chemical messages into the air that are detected by other trees. For instance, a tree under attack by insects will use a chemical message to warn nearby ones, affording them the opportunity to muster their defenses to ward off the coming assault. One if by land, two if by sea? Humans do not have a monopoly on sophisticated forms of communication.

Many nature mystics employ soulfulness, reverence, and trust toward trees, often a particular tree. And the most common ways of doing this appear to be (1) sitting beneath a tree, (2) climbing up and perching in it [again, part of our ancient hominid past], (3) soulfully communicating with it [what some may refer to as listening to and speaking with a tree], and (4) what I call "standing with the trees" (more on that shortly).

Now, when humans who largely regard the rest of nature as an "it" rather than a Thou suddenly begin subject-to-subject rather than subject-to-object interaction with the Creation, they often succumb to projection. For example, they may begin to interact with a tree almost as if it is a human-like persona in another package. While I have no way of knowing, my guess is that trees don't make this mistake about humans. This tendency to anthropomorphize other entities is longstanding in our species, even to the point that many people view God as a transcendent being that looks, more or less, like one of us.

Consequently, when we reference "talking" or "listening" to a tree, we tend to conceptualize this in human terms, not unlike two people carrying on a conversation. In contrast, nature mystics closely listen to trees in an effort to learn more about their language, so to speak. By soulfully sensing a tree, one discovers experientially (rather than conceptually) that communicating with it requires a radically different means of interaction. It is true that all entities in the Creation speak, but, so far as we know, only one does so in our language. The challenge facing a nature mystic is to listen with soul, not just mind, and to do so with sufficient openness and sensitivity that she or he begins to "hear the voice" of the other Thou, be that a tree or some other natural entity or process.

So the Way of Trees is predominately a path of listening with one's whole being, of absorbing what one experiences and feels from a tree in the hope that, gradually, its language will become discernable. And in turn, the activity of talking to a tree is primarily about communicating through a very deep channel, so to speak. While some of us try to "talk" to trees using our spoken language, it is better to let the trees teach us how to communicate with them. This is difficult to describe in words (because it operates outside of them), and will strike the typical rational mind as preposterous, but it may enlighten us to recall that legendary naturalist John Muir (think Yosemite) was in the habit of sitting with various plants in an effort to cultivate a certain rapport with them. Of trees, he wrote:

> I could distinctly hear the varying tones of individual trees—Spruce, and Fir, and Pine, and leafless Oak. Each was expressing itself in its own way, singing its own song, and making its own particular gestures . . .

So if you decide to walk the Way of Trees, then the act of surrender, of allowing the consciousness of another entity to mediate the interaction, is essential, as is the act of reverence. In my case, I don't approach a tree in this regard without silently asking its permission and indulgence. One is reminded of the Hindu tradition of bowing to another and saying "Namaste," which is roughly translated as "I honor the place in you where God dwells." The nature mystic approaches trees, and much else in the Creation, with this kind of humility and adoration.

Method

The kind of interaction I find most helpful in this regard is what I call "standing with the trees." This is simple and unobtrusive on a physical level but more demanding in both the mental and spiritual realms. My approach is to:

- Walk about until I encounter a single tree, or a cluster of them, that seems to reach for me (again, being found is important).
- Once there, I wait to be "told" where to stand. In this sense, being told often emerges as an intuitive sense of place. It is often helpful to experiment by standing in different locations near a tree or among a collection of them until one feels connected.
- Once settled in this manner, the act of standing with another sentient being becomes the central focus of soulfulness. In the same sense in which we can absorb a feeling of belonging when in the company of a group of people, so can we with a tree or trees (perhaps even more so).
- While standing, do your best to quiet the mind's incessant chatter and open your heart and soul to the presence of these kindred spirits. Be with them in the most fundamental of senses—characterized by mutual presence, silence, and a shared experience in space and time.

In this respect, I have found that, being unique entities, different species of trees and different individuals within each species impart diverse experiences of soulfulness. Listening to and being with oaks, for instance, is distinct from being with willows, tamaracks, or palms. And even among a grove of the same species, such as Douglas Firs, for example, each tree is inimitable, exuding an aura of its own nature, being, and history. I recall standing in a family of oaks in one of southern Wisconsin's now rare ecosystems called an oak savannah. After abiding with the half dozen trees that live there, I felt a strong pull toward one in particular. I spent additional time with it, sitting by its side for a while, and then placing my hands on its thick, canyoned bark. Now, I am in relation to this tree, as well as its adjacent family of kindred entities. I visit them several times each year.

When we stand with the trees, we are interacting with organisms whose lineage is far older, more finished, and complete than our own. They carry a depth of experience and wisdom that eclipses our species' brief tenure on this planet. As such, we have much to learn from them. But we shall only learn if we consent to walk the Way of Trees with deep reverence and an open soul.

Application

The Way of Trees is particularly useful when:

- You feel spiritually alone or alienated—set apart or disconnected.
- You are suffering a kind of despair about human affairs and what we are doing to the planet and our own kind. Trees seem to reassure us through their courage, persistence, and longevity.
- You feel spiritually weak, drifting, without roots or inner strength.
- You have reached the point in your spiritual work when human teachers and wisdom are no longer resonating in your soul. One requires the silent knowledge and steadfastness of older and wiser beings.

CHAPTER 8

The Way of Water

As pure water poured into pure water becomes the very same, so does the Self of the illumined man or woman verily become one with the Godhead.

—From the *Katha Upanishad*

Water.

Made from the combination of hydrogen (the most abundant gas in the cosmos) and oxygen, this remarkable substance is as close to the elixir of life as anything gets. At least life as we tend to define it.

Poets, philosophers, scientists, and mystics, not to mention every kid on the planet, have long been fascinated with water. Incredibly powerful while simultaneously yielding and mercurial, H_2O has the capacity, given time (which it freely takes), to shape entire landscapes, move mountains, and reduce solid rock to sugar sand and, eventually, dust blowing in the wind. At one moment soft and comforting, it can rapidly transform into one of the most destructive and lethal forces we encounter. Covering about 70 percent of the planet's surface and able to readily migrate from a gaseous state (water vapor) to a solid one (ice), water works in balanced harmony with the other elemental substances and forces in our world to weave and nourish the web of animate life. For example, water is critical to sustaining the Earth's benign climate. Unlike land surfaces, the oceans absorb and release solar energy slowly, helping to keep global temperatures within a narrow life-sustaining band.

All of us are familiar with the Earth's atmosphere that encompasses the gaseous orb that surrounds and protects our planet. Far fewer are aware of the hydrosphere, that which consists of all bodies of water, masses of ice, and the water vapor suspended in the air. Even if you live in an arid climate, you are in the hydrosphere, surrounded as we all are by water vapor in the atmosphere. And it is huge. In some areas of the Pacific Ocean, the hydrosphere sinks to a depth of almost seven miles beneath the Earth's surface. Speaking of which, the oceans contain over 97 percent of the hydrosphere, all in the form of saltwater. The other 3 percent, which is fresh water, is mostly ice, and over 90 percent of that is in Antarctica, followed by Greenland.

When you settle into your warm bath, plunge into that ice-cold glacial lake, or float weightless over a coral reef, you are essentially rejoining that which comprises about 65 percent of your mass. As one biologist told me, "When you go swimming, you are mainly a sack of water floating in a bigger sack of water." So it should come as little surprise that the substantive and, therefore, spiritual connection between humans and H_2O is primal. Only oxygen (a component of water) plays an equally vital role in sustaining us.

Consequently, when we embrace the Way of Water, we embrace ourselves, taking that of which we are largely composed and placing it in relationship with its source. Long regarded as the womb of organic life, water may have been the first sanctuary for Earth's earliest animate entities (perhaps bacteria-like organisms that lived near scalding hydrothermal vents deep in the ocean). In this sense, pursuing the Way of Water is essentially a journey to our primal beginnings.

In addition to our elemental bond with water, there are strong similarities in our respective attributes. Like water, humans can be warm, embracing, and nurturing while also harboring the potential to be cold, aggressive, and destructive. In kind, both entities can be placid and even stagnant, or they can manifest as moving, turbulent, and ebullient. When diverted from its natural course, such as when rivers are impeded by dams and levees, water will relentlessly seek to re-establish its intrinsic path and express its nature—much like people who are similarly stifled and imprisoned. After our species is no more, dammed rivers like the Mississippi will make quick work of our concrete and steel barriers, and cut new channels that reflect their intrinsic intentions, rather than our own.

Many of us are innately drawn to water not only for its visual and auditory beauty but also because it echoes deep in our souls. Whether at a wave-battered beach, by a cascading waterfall, or beside a murmuring brook, most of us are rapidly mesmerized by the language of water, which consists of both its graceful, fluid energy and its embracing, harmonic sound. Just as humans can stare for hours at the glowing embers of a campfire, so also do we find ourselves equally absorbed by the effortless flowing of water, be it a babbling brook, crashing waves, or a torrential waterfall. This hypnotic effect is more than a mechanical process of synaptic relaxation (so-called "white noise"). It stems from the open spiritual door that water presents to our psyches and souls. Water speaks to us because we are, for the most part, water, outward appearances to the contrary. And this inside-outside confluence whispers to us spiritually about the unity that underpins the apparent separation of material forms, ourselves included.

Of course, the same can be said of soil and air and a host of other materials and processes in our midst. However, with water this bond is more prominent and immediate. Something deep and unconscious within us looks upon water with a knowing recognition, a primal sense of kinship.

One of my best friends and a longtime backpacking companion, Mike, is a nature mystic who feels a deep affinity with water. Over the course of our many wilderness treks, he has repeatedly succumbed to "being found" by this mercurial substance in many of its permutations. Once when we were high in the Colorado Rockies, he became mesmerized by a small waterfall not far from our campsite, which was just below the tree line. He found himself repeatedly hanging out by its cascading torrent. He would sit next to it and meditate, read, collect drinking water, and just generally abide in its presence.

"When are you going to get under this waterfall?" I asked him one afternoon when I joined him there.

"I can't get in that water," he insisted. "It's mostly runoff from snowmelt. I mean, this water is just above freezing."

But the twinkle in his eyes spoke for a part of him that didn't buy it. And neither did I.

"You'll be going in," I proclaimed. "It's just a matter of time."

Sure enough, on our final day at that site, he got naked and thrust himself directly under the fall. His loud whoops echoed down the long valley sloping away from our lofty perch. When he emerged, cold, wet, and renewed, he was bathed in the kind of emotional elation and sensory exquisiteness that nature mystics experience when they are in their element.

While very much a water person myself, Mike has always seemed on the lunatic fringe in this regard. On several occasions, he has persuaded me to join him in these immersions with the Way of Water, but he has also ventured into rivers, lakes, and ocean surf that, while beautiful, seemed more than my body could withstand. Nonetheless, during one of our backpacks along Pictured Rocks National Lakeshore in Michigan's Upper Peninsula, he convinced me to take the plunge into Lake Superior's icy depths. It gave new meaning to the phrase, "Lose your mind and come to your senses." Of the many natural elements and settings that can sufficiently engage one's senses so as to quiet or even silence the thinking mind, water is among the most potent. And in Mike's case, it is part of his "naturality," a concept we will explore in the next chapter.

In my role as a nature therapist (a psychotherapist who uses nature interaction to promote emotional healing), I have worked with many individuals who have used water for cleansing rituals. One salient example is a middle-aged gentleman who had made a considerable mess of his personal life, despite being quite successful in his career. Following the demise of his twenty-some-year marriage, he found himself soiled with regret and self-reproach, literally spending hours thinking about all his past mistakes and, as he put it, "stupid decisions." While he made sincere apologies and amends to those he had wronged, the self-recriminations emanating from his psyche would not subside.

During our talk therapy sessions, we strolled in a natural area adjacent to my office, one that had a stream flowing through it. Frequently, he would ask that we "go sit by that stream and talk." Eventually, I suggested he consider "washing away" some of his guilt and remorse with a water ritual, and he agreed. Again adhering to the principle of being found, he set about visiting a variety of rivers, lakes, and creeks in search of one that would connect strongly with his spirit. Before long, he found himself "chosen" by a fast-running brook with crystal clear water coursing over a sandy bottom.

It was later in autumn, and I suggested he collect some dried leaves (which "found" him) to use in the ritual itself. On each leaf he wrote a single word representing one of the many miscues and misdeeds that bedeviled his conscience. Then, on a day of his choosing, we went to the brook, leaves in hand, to conduct his cleansing ceremony. After sitting by the water for a time, practicing soulfulness and setting an intention for the ritual, he was ready. Despite the chill, he stripped down to a bathing suit, waded into the water and, one by one, released the leaves into the shimmering flow, taking time to watch each one disappear downstream. Then, tears streaming down his face, he kneeled in the water, scooped some up in his cupped hands, and released it over his head. He repeated this several times until his hair and face were wetted down and water cascaded in rivulets down his chest and back. His tears and those of the brook became one, and he surrendered his pain to the Creation.

Method

The Way of Water can be sought in many fashions. Some include:

- Being found by water simply involves placing one's self in its presence. Many of us have access to a beach, lake, pond, wetland, waterfall, river, brook, field of snow, or even fountain that affords this contact. Some put small waterfalls or fountains in their homes or offices. Others simply go for a walk in the rain or mist, in the snow, or on a frozen pond (check for safety).
- As always, engaging in sensory awareness is key. For many, touching water is as salient (or more so) than watching or listening to it. Don't

be afraid to get wet, whether by walking in the rain, lying in the snow, or plunging into an ocean, lake, or river (again, be safe). When in graduate school, I lived for a time in a farmhouse in Iowa. A nearby field held a fast-running stream shaded by overarching trees. When the stream ran particularly high, I would immerse myself in it while clinging to an overhanging branch. Suspended in this manner, my body floated just below the surface, my torso and legs flowing with the strong current like a submerged reed. If such immersions seem a bit much, simply use your hands or feet to get the feel of it.

- Use water as part of ritual action (a ceremonial behavior that invokes spiritual meaning) to promote a dialogue with nature. Most of us are familiar with baptism as a sacrament in the Christian religion where water is employed to spiritually cleanse and anoint a person into the "Kingdom of God." Also, in the Roman Catholic tradition, water is blessed by a priest to make it holy and, then, used by devotees in making the sign of the cross. While applying water as a symbol is both meaningful and appropriate, this substance is also a spiritual entity in its own right, not just a symbol for something else. In many religious traditions, a symbol or icon is used to stand for something separate and distinct from itself. Among nature mystics, a symbol also has innate meaning—it is a spiritual presence in its own right, even when used to focus consciousness on something else (such as love, courage, transformation, etc.). Consequently, if one uses water as part of a ritual act of spiritual cleansing, it not only invokes a symbolic power greater than itself, but also brings to bear its own essence as a manifestation of the Creation.

Application

The Way of Water flows well when:

- You feel very much like a thing, an object devoid of essence, life, and verve.
- A feeling of being stuck and unchangeable has taken hold of your soul.
- You want to experience a "washing away" of leftover memories, feelings, or attitudes that are hobbling your emotional well-being or impeding your spiritual development.
- A sense of emotional or spiritual flow is already occurring inside you, and there is a desire to express this more outwardly or to amplify its intensity.

CHAPTER 9

Your Naturality

Forests, lakes, and rivers, clouds and winds, stars and flowers, stupendous glaciers and crystal snowflakes—every form of animate or inanimate existence, leaves its impress upon the soul of man.
—Orison Swett Marden

I love to think of nature as an unlimited broadcasting station through which God speaks to us every hour, if we will only tune in.
—George Washington Carver

I'm a person of the gloaming, the short but mysterious time just between day and night. Slightly different than dusk, the gloaming is when you can't quite discern whether it is night or day. It is an interlude, a transition so subtle that it defies our ability to describe it in words. It carries with it a spiritual ambience and message . . . at least for me.

And then there's autumn, the season that sings loudest to my spirit. No, not even the creative exuberance of spring or basking warmth of summer can compete with the crisp, deeply colorful, poignant days and nights of what we correctly term "the fall." It is that, indeed, but in ways far greater than simply leaves floating to the ground, lovely as they are. As the term "fall" implies at this deeper level, it is when life begins to turn toward the little death, the winter of sleep and rest, itself laying the foundation for the rebirth of life with the Sun's return.

Part of discovering our own wisdom, as individuals and as a species, is to begin to recognize who we truly are. Discovering that requires more than a grasp of psychology, sociology, and the other pedagogies that attempt to define what it means to be human. It necessitates perceiving your own inward nature by connecting with its outward manifestations in nature itself. Just as we sometimes contemplate our biological or adoptive parents, looking for clues to our own character and destiny, so too can we discover who we are by where we came from—the vast material and spiritual sea we call the Creation.

But how? Well, it can help to ask ourselves a few things.

For one, what time of day are you?

I don't mean in the "I'm a morning person" way, as in when your energy is peaking or you're at your emotional best. What time of day is most reflective of your true self? If you can readily feel your answer without having to analyze it too much, then you likely already have a deep spiritual connection to that particular set of moments—the darkest of the night, the crack of sunshine in the morning, the stunning illumination of the afternoon, or some other temporal space between. Once you feel that answer, then you have discovered a door, a way into the presence of the Creator and, by association, into your own soul.

And you have other doors. They have been with you a long time, but perhaps residing just a short way outside your conscious awareness. Let's consider another.

For instance, what season are you?

I'm not referring to your best color scheme for making a fashion statement. I am not even asking which is your favorite. My question is what season, or subset of one, best resonates with and reflects your deepest self? If you already know, if the answer came to you in a poignant memory, a quick visual image, or simply a heartfelt sense of certainty, then you have identified another potential door. Granted, the door afforded by a season is relatively brief and comes only once a year, but some of us harbor more than one. And for those who don't, that one season affords an opportunity to go on a pilgrimage or spirit quest, conduct nature-based rituals or ceremonies, or simply spend more time with the Creation.

And there are many other potential attributes of the natural world that may find resonance in your own inner nature. Some of the questions I sometimes ask folks in this regard include:

- What is your inner topography? Is it a prairie, rain forest, rugged canyon, wetland, river valley, desert, mountain, or some other environment?
- Do you have what indigenous peoples called a "spirit animal" or a "helping spirit?" Do you possess a compelling spiritual affinity for a particular creature? Have you had interactions or encounters in nature that suggest an existing kinship between you and another type of animal or life form?

- What is your inner weather? Are you sunny, overcast, storm-tossed, warm, cool, arid, humid, windy, calm, etc.?
- What sort of cloud are you? A towering thunderhead full of sound and fury? An elegant, wispy cirrus (think mare's tail) ghosting high in the sky? A dark and brooding overcast? The Earth-hugging cloud we call fog?

When I've put these kinds of questions to people who attend nature's ways workshops, many seem puzzled at first. After all, we are trained to assess who we are primarily on the basis of psychological nomenclature. Each of us has a personality, we are told, and it is comprised of particular traits, attitudes, emotional tendencies, and the like. We use words like optimistic, melancholy, intense, assertive, passive, self-reliant, perfectionist, and scores of others to describe characteristics of one's self that, in aggregate, supposedly constitute your identity.

However, among nature mystics, something I call "naturality" is a more useful and, in my view, accurate way to determine one's unique psychological and spiritual pedigree. This is not a great leap. After all, without realizing it, many of us already refer to someone's naturality in attempting to describe her or his personality. We banter about terms like a "sunny disposition" or a "hothead" or a "lone wolf" or a "dirty rat," among many others, in reference to someone's inner temperament and personal attributes. In a largely unconscious fashion, we already grasp the connections between who we are on the inside and what we are part of on the outside.

In some indigenous cultures, particularly among Native Americans, tribal members were often named in this fashion. There was a culturally endorsed recognition that what we now refer to as someone's personality is reflective of particular aspects of the Creation itself. Anyone who has watched the movie *Dances with Wolves* has a basic understanding of this tradition. Names such as Crazy Horse, Snake Maiden, Sitting Bull, Star Dancer, Blackhawk, Rippling Water, Returning Moon, and many others, were chosen to convey a person's naturality and inner spirit.

In my work as a nature therapist, I often forgo the terse lexicon of psychology, including its approach to personality assessment, in favor of determining a person's naturality. Overall, this process is received very positively by most people, often because it affords them a richer and more meaningful way to understand themselves and how they fit with the larger order of things. While some struggle with this concept at first, once they begin to recognize how aspects of their inner nature are reflected in entities and processes in the natural world, they usually make the conceptual transition in short order.

I recall a young woman who sought my ministrations because, despite considerable effort to do so, she had no clear sense of her own identity. She had seen therapists before, only to have them assign her labels such as "passive" and "dependent" and "anxious." Nonetheless, she came away from these diagnostic encounters thinking, "I don't know who I am." This is not an uncommon lament among the young, but for her, this fuzziness had persisted too long.

"If you don't know who you are, it's hard to determine what you want or how you should conduct yourself," I suggested, and she quite agreed.

We mutually determined to set aside the psychobabble and seek greater clarity about her inner nature by exposing her to the larger Creation. A series of "homework" assignments for her included both forays into safe natural areas, gardens, and parks, as well as time spent with videos, educational programs, photography, and books focused on nature. The intention was to determine if certain experiences or observations elicited any "Aha!" moments, those that often reflect an innate association between one's inner attributes and external aspects in the natural realm. They did.

She began describing her naturality as aligned with early spring, mist, fields of closed flowers, choppy water, and, most surprisingly to her, butterflies. Intellectually, she assigned several interpretations to these aspects of her naturality, including:

Early spring:	Not quite fully born. Still in the process of becoming.
Mist:	Shrouded in confusion. Waiting for the rising Sun to "burn it off."
Closed flowers:	Inner beauty, but protecting itself from the world. Waiting until conditions are right (Sun and warmth) before bursting forth.
Choppy water:	Driven by an inner "wind" full of nascent energy, but still confined, creating considerable inner tension. Likely a manifestation of what she called "anxiety."
Butterflies:	Gentle, seeking sweetness, and part of the web of life.

Not only did these associations, which came to her intuitively, afford a clearer and more reassuring sense of self, but they also proved instructive. Recognizing that these aspects of her naturality afforded potential "doors" to a deeper-felt-understanding of her own nature in relation to the Creation, she was able to use them accordingly. In contrast, for example, being told she was "passive" was far less illuminating or helpful than feeling like "closed flowers."

Rather than tackling her presumed passivity (which carries a clear negative connotation), she set about working with the doorway afforded by flowers and, subsequently, became a gardener, both in and out of doors. Before long, she had become an accomplished grower of flowers, an activity that soothed her choppy water, moved her further into spring, and aligned her with her helping spirit, the butterfly. These tangible while also symbolic actions (working with soil, sunlight, plants, etc.) aligned her inner nature with the spiritual power and élan vital of nature on the outside. Without realizing it, she was gradually altering her naturality by working with the transformative strength of the life force (growing new life).

In our highly psychological culture, it is common to assign people certain symptoms, diagnostic labels, personality traits, and other abstract descriptors that lump them into broad and stereotypic groupings based on comparisons to presumed societal norms. Once so assigned, individuals are told whether their personality characteristics are healthy or dysfunctional and, if the latter, what can be done to "get fixed." That there are people, often those with serious mental illnesses, who benefit from this process is beyond dispute. But for countless others, it offers nothing more than conceptual definitions based on abstract premises. In contrast, my clients who discover their naturality usually report that this provides them a far clearer and more positive understanding of who they are, why they are here, how they are connected to the Creation, and how best to remain true to themselves.

What's more, identifying a person's naturality also increases the probability that she or he will recognize the broader spiritual context in which psychological, emotional, and interpersonal concerns are played out. If I define myself as an anxious person, for instance, this binds who I am to narrow and often reductionistic explanations and meanings associated with my state of being, such as disordered brain chemistry, maladaptive learning, dysfunctional coping mechanisms, and the like. Alternatively, if I discover an innate affinity between how I feel inside or my identity and some aspect of nature that speaks to me—in this example, perhaps a gusting wind, a thunderstorm, or hummingbird—then my "issues" or sense of self are linked with a far greater whole (the Creation), as well as with other kindred entities or processes that reflect a similar nature to my own. The results? I feel less alone and isolated. I can recognize my challenges as part of a greater and more spiritual framework that is "natural." And frequently, my symptoms become less like enemies and more like teachers.

If you want to truly know yourself, follow nature's ways.

Over time, your naturality will emerge.

Through the mirrors of the Creation, you will learn to see yourself.

CHAPTER 10

The Way of Stones

Our life, exempt from public haunt, finds tongues in trees, books in the running brooks, sermons in stones, and good in everything.
—William Shakespeare, *As You Like It*

Stones hold the memories of the Earth.
—Native American Aphorism

For many, the Way of Stones seems just about the opposite of the Way of Wind or Water. And it feels like a far cry from the Way of Trees as well.

Rocks, stones, boulders—not the warm, fuzzy, flowing, and majestic entities that draw many to nature. Nevertheless, like trees, stones occupy a deep remembrance in the lineage of our kind. The so-called Stone Age began almost two million years ago when human-like primates first employed rocks as tools and, perhaps, weapons. For many peoples, it largely ended around 2500 BCE, although there were notable exceptions. Throughout that immense span of time, our ancestors were very focused on stones and came to know them intimately. They represented partners in our quest for greater technology and empowered us with a decided edge in the contest for survival.

Many modern humans retain a strong but largely unconscious attraction to stones and rocks. Most visibly, we adorn ourselves in a variety of precious gems and ornamental minerals, incorporating them into rings, bracelets, necklaces, and broaches, to name a few. Although the Stone Age is long gone, we continue to employ an array of rocks in buildings and monuments. From polished marble to raw fieldstones, we have integrated these dense, weighty condensations of matter (slow energy, some might say) into modern architectural and construction practices. Less ostentatiously, many people are rock collectors and a small but consequential commerce has emerged in this regard. Unfortunately, the private and sometimes illegal market for fossils, aesthetic minerals, and even petroglyphs (carvings by ancient peoples on stone facings) has left frequent scares on our wild landscapes. Less destructively, many children squirrel away amateur rock collections, mostly those they find on their own or that are gifted by an older family member. Among those individuals and families that maintain a nature table in their homes and among nature mystics who keep small indoor shrines, stones are ubiquitous additions.

Most rocks are classified by geologists as "aggregates," meaning they are combinations of one or more minerals. In many cases, these minerals are so tiny and imperceptible that the rocks appear to be homogenous hunks of dense material without discernible differentiations. However, were you to examine a slice of such rock under a microscope, you would see grains of minerals, often a variety of them. Particularly fascinating are sedimentary rocks, such as coal. These consist of matter (and energy) that was once in the form of older rocks, plants, or animals, and that accumulated in layers of loose material that, over eons, hardened into a new form. Sedimentary rock reminds us of the powerful forces of transformation at work within what many perceive as the inert matter that makes up most of the planet. Stones change more slowly than we humans, but they are alive and in transmutation, just like us. In fact, geologists use the term "metamorphism" to describe the process by which rocks and stones change forms, including size, shape, and chemical composition.

In fact, with a few exceptions, the entire rocky crust of our planet has been continuously (albeit very slowly) recycled through a process called "subduction." The tectonic plates that make up the continents and the ocean floors are engaged in a kind of perpetual slow motion collision (moving about four inches a year) that drives the surface (the crust and outermost mantle) deep into the Earth. Some tectonic plates are also diverging, meaning that previously buried rocky is being brought to the surface, most often under the oceans (although you can see this in Iceland). These moving and recycling plates vary in thickness from about five miles (under the ocean) to almost 120 miles (under some continents). There are a few places, primarily in Greenland and Australia, where surface rocks have remained exposed for extremely long periods, perhaps since they first formed on the early primordial Earth.

Why the attraction to rocks?

Like many of the essentially unconscious pulls we feel toward entities, objects, and processes in nature, I believe the Way of Stones calls to us. Referencing again the latent potential for an I-Thou dialogue between humans and their natural environment, these kinds of instinctive attractions may represent doorways to the Creation, calling quietly to our souls in the hope we will enter. In this sense, when you are strolling along a rocky path or beach, you may sometimes notice that your attention is "grabbed" by a stone. You may tell yourself that this is simply because there is something about its shape or color that you find appealing. And while this is true at one level, it is important to remember that, while rock in its various manifestations—stones, boulders, sand, etc.—does not seem alive to us, it is made of the same elemental stuff as we and the rest of the cosmos. A Native American adage tells us that, "A stone breathes once every thousand years." While perhaps not literally true (who knows?), this metaphor speaks to the aliveness of the entire Creation.

Unlike some other natural entities, stones have the capacity to become companions of sorts. My sister, Florence, who is a poet and nature mystic, gave me a stone from the Yellow Medicine River in southwestern Minnesota. This stone found her while she was walking near the river's bank, communing with the Creation and, after keeping it for some time, she decided it needed to be with me. It has been now, for over a decade, primarily riding on the console of my car. Whenever I interact with it, either by touch or sight, I feel a renewed connection with the Great Plains from which it came, as well as the Yellow Medicine River itself. In moments of immersion in soulfulness, this stone "speaks" to me in its own language, and I do my best to listen. Of course, it does not tell me things in words or in the manner that humans communicate. Rather, it conveys a sense of itself, its relative timelessness, ancient past and long future, and of the billions of years of cosmic churning that gave it form in this time and place. The Creation has a way of whispering to us about such matters, provided we lend an ear, or a soul.

Some of us keep stones (or, perhaps, are kept by them) to rekindle memories or spark states of awareness. As a child, I had a small chunk of quartz that resided in a pocket of my jeans. This stone and I first came together when we encountered each other beneath the surface of that sacred (to me) lake I mentioned in northern Illinois. I had been snorkeling on a rock-strewn sandbar when we spotted each other. Glistening as it did in the sun-pierced water, I snatched it from the bottom—the beginning of our long association. Until I became too cool to carry it around (think adolescence), we were frequent companions. I recall how, in moments of duress, I would reach in my pocket and slowly run my fingers over its irregular, sometimes sharp surface. In some manner that makes sense only to a child or a nature mystic, that stone and I were friends, and its presence afforded me a measure of comfort and reassurance. There is, of course, nothing rational about such a relationship, as is true of any spiritual bond and more than a few human ones.

The Way of Stones is particularly applicable to symbolic or ritual actions that address challenging emotional states or existential conundrums, and it is equally helpful in creating spiritual ceremonies involving nature interaction.

For example, a thirty-something career woman I'll call Jennie sought my guidance because she was bedeviled with a chronic sense of anxiety that seemed existential in origin. This kind of dread is often referred to as "angst," and it differs from fears and apprehensions that arise in relation to specific situations (e.g., public speaking, flying, etc.) or phobic stimuli (e.g., spiders, elevators, etc.). In contrast, existential angst is a sort of pervasive insecurity about life and one's self in relation to it. It is characterized by a persistent underlying feeling of peril and uncertainty, often without knowing why. Unlike situational or object-specific anxiety, the existential variety is more of a spiritual issue than a purely psychological or emotional one.

In this regard, Jennie seemed a good candidate for using the Way of Stones on a symbolic level. At my urging, she went on a series of walks on a rocky beach and was eventually found by a stone that seemed to visually symbolize her chronic dread. The stone itself was a dark and gnarly composite of minerals congealed in an asynchronous and jagged pattern.

"This represents how I feel," she told me, the stone in hand.

"Good. Now we need you to be found by a stone that symbolizes how you hope to feel," I suggested.

After a few more "hoping to be found" strolls, Jennie returned with another stone that depicted what she longed for—a sense of being grounded, more at peace, and solid. Interestingly, it still had small segments of knotty, incongruous components, but these were set inside a smooth, undulating stone that felt heavy, snug, and pleasing in her closed fist. In explaining how this entity reflected her hoped-for inner state, she said, "A little angst can be a helpful thing sometimes, so I don't want to erase it totally, but I do want it to be part of a greater sense of peace."

Next, Jennie needed to determine how to use her newly formed I-Thou relationship with these stones to further her spiritual transformation from dread to trust. Rather than imposing my own ideas, I encouraged her to bring both stones home, place them at her bedside where she could touch/see them each morning upon waking and every evening before sleep, and wait for some sense of direction to emerge. Soon, she felt an intuitive urge to have both stones accompany here during her daily routines. Subsequently, when she became very anxious she would hold the "angst stone" in one hand and the "trust stone" in the other, an approach she later described as "balancing." After a few days, her symbolic ritual shifted. Each morning, she would place both stones in one hand, hold them to her heart, and then put the angst stone down at her bedside while taking the trust stone with her for the rest of the day.

Finally, she began to perform nature rituals with the stones. She took them to a favorite river near her home (Way of Place), one that was relatively small but fast running and clear. As before, she would hold both stones to her heart, but then she placed the one representing her angst in the river, steadying it on a large, flat rock just beneath the surface. She described this to me as a "cleansing" action, one designed to help soothe and wash away her dread. In this sense, the stone became a vicarious but spiritually connected aspect of her inner self. Because of their spiritually formed bond, what happened to the stone also reverberated inside her spirit. As it was cleansed and soothed, so was she, symbolically. Using that term—"symbolically"—does not mean that this ceremonial action was some sort of pretense. When soulfully connected with an aspect of the Creation, we are experiencing an interaction between two forms of energy—in this instance, rock and human. Through this process, each influences the other, and transformation becomes possible.

Gradually, and in a manner neither of us could entirely explain, Jennie began to feel more "solid," as she put, which then led to a sense of being less easily rattled and more at peace. With her dread slowly subsiding, she grew more trusting and open toward life. And the stones?

"You said that stones carry the memory of the Earth," she told me. "Well, now they carry the memories of me, of my struggle. We'll be hanging out together for a long time, I'd guess."

The Way of Stones, then, is a bit different than some of the other paths followed by nature mystics. Our association with these entities, like that with trees, takes on more of an individual-to-individual quality, something less evident in interactions with wind or water, for example. And it is, in some sense, portable. Stones can readily be brought inside, kept over long periods, and placed in different locations in one's personal topography. This is not as true for large rocks, of course, although they also afford unique relationships. There is a small boulder in my backyard prairie garden that my son and I inadvertently unearthed while digging a flowerbed close to our house. We laboriously rolled it to the prairie garden, where it now sits among the coneflowers, prairie dock, and compass plants. And on occasion, I sit on it to feel more closely connected with the planet. Nonetheless, stones are well suited to rituals and symbolic actions involving nature's ways.

Method

- One approach to the Way of Stones involves being found by and sitting on a large rock or boulder, doing so not simply for repose but also to feel against one's skin the sinew of the Earth. Not surprisingly, this affords both a physical and spiritual sense of being grounded, of a solid connection with the planet (which is largely composed of the raw materials that go into rocks), and with the energy innervating all things, no matter how inert or lifeless they may seem on first inspection. Entering a state of soulfulness in this manner affords a unique experience far different from that with water, wind, trees, and the like.

- Another is based on "being found" by a stone. If this occurs, it is respectful to honor this invitation by incorporating the stone into your life in some meaningful fashion. I am not speaking of being a rock hound, but rather of employing stones as symbols and using them in rituals (as Jennie did). There are many symbolic and ritual actions that are enhanced through soulful interaction with stones. They particularly lend themselves to ceremonies that focus on: (1) representing the invisible, such as emotions, attitudes, and states of consciousness in a tangible form; (2) transforming inner states through ceremonial action, such as letting go of anger, grief, despair, fear, etc.; (3) reminding one's self of meaningful events, goals, purposes, and ideals.

Application

The Way of Stones is highly applicable when:

- You are feeling ungrounded, scattered, confused, or existentially adrift.
- You feel hyperactive, "wired," or "coming apart."
- You are challenging the engrained perspective that only so-called organic life forms are truly alive and that other "things," such as air, water, and rock, are inert.
- You are grappling with vexing-but-difficult-to-pin-down states of awareness or moods that may become more evident and more readily transformed through symbolic or ritual action.

CHAPTER 11

The Way of Wind

Forget not that the earth delights to feel your bare feet, and the winds long to play with your hair.

—Kahlil Gibran

While astrophysicists now talk about the entire cosmos being permeated by a kind of energy-based atmosphere called the "cosmic background radiation," or CBR, let us concern ourselves with something closer to home—the Earth's atmosphere. Like you and I, the Earth breathes. When you walk outside and feel the wind brushing over your face, hair, and skin, you are immersed in the respiratory rhythm of our planet. Our atmosphere extends about 70 miles above the Earth's surface and buffers us from lethal ultraviolet and cosmic rays, not to mention showers of small meteors and other space debris. It also regulates temperature, humidity, and other life-sustaining processes. Without it, our planet would be a relatively barren orb with an average temperature hovering below minus 50 degrees Fahrenheit.

That's the big picture, but trapped as we are in our little sectors on the planetary grid, we are inclined to mentally compartmentalize the atmosphere, imagining that the dry, hot winds of America's desert southwest are unrelated to the humidity of Africa's equatorial jungles, or the frigid chills blasting atop the Antarctic ice shelf. In fact, the Earth's orb of air is one continuous system, flowing in currents and eddies much like the oceans that occupy most of the planet's surface, and not unlike the air circulating in and out of your lungs. As such, it is a unified process that, like the physicists' underlying quantum energy field, is characterized by variations or ripples that manifest as seemingly distinct local conditions.

The wind is a consequence of the uneven distribution of heat in the bubble of air surrounding the Earth. This lumpy thermal allotment creates differences in atmospheric pressure (which we measure with barometers), and the air constantly strives to equalize these disparities by flowing away from areas of higher pressure and toward areas of lower pressure. This is the same vector you see when water flows downward (from its high) into a whirlpool (toward its low). This is the genesis of the wind, and even when it seems calm, the air is always moving.

Consequently, one door that can open to a mystical awareness of nature is through sensory immersion in the wind, the rhythm of the Earth's breath. This creates soulful interaction with a process that, in itself, is a microcosm of the patterns of flowing energy in the cosmos. Viewing the substrate of matter and energy in the universe as a quantum field (as many physicists do), as a dynamic and ever-changing sea of vibrations and intersecting patterns, it is easy to recognize how closely the wind is aligned with this fundamental process. As such, it strikes a deep chord in the soul, reminding us of the flowing energy that innervates our existence.

The Way of Wind is deceptively simple. It can be embraced virtually anywhere in the natural world, although it seems helpful to seek a location where human sounds and smells are reduced or absent. Ideally, such a place will include some other natural entity that is already in harmony with the wind, such as trees, water, tall grasses, or even powdery snow. Closer to home, some folks use wind chimes, banners, or socks.

As always, finding the right spot is an intuitive undertaking. Rather than being too analytic about it, simply walk into a copasetic area and wander or look about until some location finds you (draws you to it). Once there, again follow your intuition about whether to stand or sit, and feel free to play with getting situated in a comfortable position. Once a sense of "it feels right" takes hold, you are ready to look for the door that opens through the Way of Wind.

The first step is to employ sensory-based awareness (soulfulness) in order to quiet your thinking mind and awaken your senses. The Earth's respirations can be felt, smelled (even tasted, some say), heard, and often indirectly seen. Even the stillest of days can engage most of one's senses. So turn them on. Spend a bit of time with each one (sight, sound, smell, touch), focusing your awareness through the lens of each sensory modality.

As we've examined previously, in seeking the Way of Wind or any other of nature's ways, you will probably suffer the interference of your thinking mind. It helps little to make war on one's thoughts by straining to suppress them. However, the Way of Wind provides a unique and powerful avenue for getting out of the monkey cage of thinking, thinking, and more thinking.

For example, one can visually imagine one's thoughts as ethereal forms (like sky-writing suspended in one's mind) that are dissipated and blown away by the wind. Or one can mentally "place" thoughts in one's open hands and then, motioning upward and away, release them into the sky.

Once your thoughts have been quieted and a certain degree of sensing has occurred, it is often helpful to enter the experience of the Earth's breath through one's physical movements. For instance, in a strong steady wind, you can bend with the flow of the air, much as a tall blade of grass or a willow tree. As you do, you may notice that there is an ebb and flow to the rush of the atmosphere, that there are gusts followed by relative pauses. By blending your physical movements with these natural rhythms, you more fully enter the Way of Wind, even to the point where you and the air are dancing in harmony.

In point of fact, you are already participating in the Earth's respiratory cycles. Taking in oxygen and other gasses and releasing carbon dioxide, which itself is absorbed by other entities, particularly plants and the seas, makes you a small element in a vast and complex tapestry of interactions that constitute the breathing of our world. By consciously entering the Way of Wind, you are simply tuning your awareness toward a participatory process that goes unrecognized by most of us much of the time. This is an act of both spiritual consciousness-raising and reverence.

I recall a warm spring afternoon when I sought the Way of Wind. My quest took me into a forest of stately oaks and maples. It was an interlude between rainstorms that had showered the landscape on and off throughout the day. All the plants were bursting in fresh greens, glistening with moisture, and swaying to the ebb and flow of robust southwesterly gusts. Wandering for a time, I was found by a hilltop that afforded a broad view of the trees. There I experienced convergence with the Earth's breath in a most exquisite manner.

It was a synergistic sensory immersion, one encompassing (1) the sound of the wind surfing through the forest canopy in tumbling ebbs followed by cascading flows; (2) the feel of the warm and moist air rushing over my skin and, at times, tossing my frame a bit off center; (3) the sight of the trees swaying in slow, surf-like cadence, like a crowd of majestic sentinels moving in harmony with the inhalation and exhalation of a far greater being; and (4) the penetrating aroma of the lush greenery and pregnant soil swirling on convective foils like mist spiraling in a storm. Like the trees, my body swayed, dancing to the traversing rhythms engulfing my consciousness. The proprioceptive sensation of being a separate, walled-off entity slipped away, and I experienced myself drifting with and then dissolving into the planetary respiration.

When an elderly gentleman sought my guidance in following nature's ways, he already recognized his strong intuitive attraction to the wind. A lifelong sailor, private pilot, and kite flyer, his bond with the Earth's breath had been apparent since his youth. Nonetheless, his specific request may seem a tad odd to some.

"I want to learn to disappear," he told me, a somewhat mischievous smile on his face.

"In what sense?" I asked.

"Well, I'm going to meet my maker soon, and I think I'd better prepare myself for that. So I want to start feeling less like a material thing and more like . . . well, like just pure energy," he explained.

It didn't require much imagination to realize that following the Way of Wind was well suited to what he sought. Wind is, fundamentally, energy in motion, and it is invisible. Sometimes, we can see what it does, but we can't actually see it. So we worked together to devise several ritual actions that would help him "disappear," at least within the confines of his own awareness. One of these required what most would consider a blustery day, with wind speeds in excess of, say, 15 miles per hour. Although, as he put it, "the stronger the better." The ritual action we concocted was quite simple. He merely went to a high and open hilltop not far from his home. Once there, he stood facing the wind, arms wide open and eyes closed, and then felt the air, as he put, "blowing through me." This act of soulful immersion with the Way of Wind had a palpable impact on his consciousness.

"I can feel more like what I really am," he told me later. "Energy. And that's how I want to feel when I leave this world."

The other ritual action involved a symbolic letting go of past worries, regrets, and painful memories. Taking pieces of fine parchment, he wrote down his cares and woes, one to a page, and then burned each one separately, collecting the ashes in individual packets. Before conducting each of his "blowing in the wind" rituals, he began by taking the ashes from one of his pages of parchment and releasing them to the wind and sky.

"Gotta lighten up if I want to be energy," he told me with a wry smile.

The Way of Wind, then, can be an exhilarating mystical interlude encompassing (a) soulfulness, (b) reverence for the Creation, and (c) surrender to and harmony with a highly dynamic natural process.

Method

To review, the Way of Wind involves:

- Being found by a location in nature.
- Reducing one's pesky thoughts (if present) by ritually releasing them to the wind.
- Engaging all one's senses to create soulfulness with the wind and air.

- "Dancing" with the wind by moving with it physically.
- Using the wind as a partner for spiritual rituals and ceremonies.

Application

The Way of Wind flows well in these circumstances:

- You are feeling spiritually stuck, weighed down, or inert.
- You feel emotionally "heavy," smothered by worries, or spiritually suffocating.
- Your body is experienced as tight, rigid, or awkward in movement.
- You are feeling a sense of physical lightness, emotional joy, and expressive spontaneity, but there is a desire to go still further into a state of flowing.

As a final side note, following the Way of Wind can make a nature mystic stand out. If you employ the "dancing" aspect of this process and there is another Homo sapiens about, he or she may well take notice. In the absence of music and a socially endorsed venue, what appears to be extemporaneous dancing is generally viewed with wariness or amusement in Western culture. What's more, even in the absence of inquiring minds, many of us feel inhibited about moving our bodies in confluence with the wind. Nonetheless, adding this kinetic element to following the Way of Wind can substantially enhance the mystical consciousness that it sometimes affords. We will examine this further in the Way of Being (chapter 18).

In other words, consider taking a chance. After all, the part of you that is being intimidated by the possibility of embarrassment (your ego) is the same part you are deliberately seeking to quiet and transcend.

Don't let it run the show.

Like the wind, let yourself flow.

CHAPTER 12

The Way of Walking

Perhaps the truth depends on a walk around the lake.
—Wallace Stevens

Why rush? Our final destination will only be the graveyard.
—Thich Nhat Hanh

I only went out for a walk, and finally concluded to stay out till sundown, for going out, I found, was really going in.
—John Muir

The Way of Walking is not as simple as it sounds.

The act of walking echoes strongly in our collective memory. After all, this capability—locomotion on two feet—changed the destiny of hominids, of which we are the only remaining species. We were able to leave the rain forests, where trees sheltered and sustained us, and push on to new environments, eventually populating the globe. What's more, becoming bipedal freed our hands for other endeavors, most notably the development and use of tools. Later, this freedom led to painting, writing, pottery, weaving, and a plethora of other creative pursuits.

Walking in a natural setting for the purpose of connecting with the spiritual atmosphere of a place is not that common. Granted, many people take walks outdoors, but most do so for other purposes. Couples and families walk as a form of social interaction and shared experience, a bonding activity. Individuals often walk for exercise and the physical/emotional high that exertion in fresh air often provides. And of course, many walk just to get there, having a clear destination in mind and proceeding with all possible dispatch.

I am reminded of this during many of my treks in the wilds. When I meet others on a backcountry trail, they are often simply passing through, rather than being present. Even some fellow backpackers I encounter during my extended wilderness quests have the countenance of a person on a mission. It is true, then, that many people—perhaps most—walk *through* the woods (or any natural setting). They do not walk *in* the woods.

The Way of Walking is certainly about being *in* a place. But it is even more. It involves being *with* a place. And while that place represents the here-and-now (a cresting wave of the life force surging through time and space), it is also an echo of the there-and-then. That may seem a contradictory assertion given the intense emphasis among nature mystics on living in the moment. However, when we walk in a soulful manner in the presence of nature, we also experience the resonance of an ancient lineage in our species. We make contact with the deep, collective memory of our forebears who, quite literally, found their feet and began to stride upright. Species memory is as real for us as for those other animate creatures to whom we somewhat condescendingly ascribe the attribute of instinct. The Way of Walking is both soulful and instinctive. It reconnects us with something we know and remember, not consciously, but buried within our DNA, the material codification of our species' shared wisdom.

Many who soulfully pursue the Way of Walking report experiencing a kind of primal sense of their animal nature, which is an aspect of what I term "naturality." This becomes most discernible when one is naked but, alas, there is little opportunity for that anymore, even in the wilds. While many travelers in the backcountry, in particular, find skinny dipping perfectly acceptable, most draw the line at skinny walking. Nevertheless, those who are so inclined and have access to what is oddly termed a "nude beach" (I thought all beaches were nude), can experience yet another dimension to the Way of Walking.

When soulfully exercised, the Way of Walking turns off the higher cognitive functions, like abstract thought, returning one's psyche to an earlier epoch in our evolution. We become more the animal and less the embodied brain.

"I felt like an ancient human walking through the primeval forest," one aspiring nature mystic told me.

The Way of Walking reacquaints us (physically, not conceptually) with a time in the history of our species when we were profoundly connected to the Creation, before our technology distanced us from our home in the natural realm. This is not a projective delusion. It is a felt knowledge drawn from a memory bank that is not the province of an individual sequestered in her or his epoch, but of an entire lineage of creatures stretching back to a past that disappears into the abyss of time itself. This felt-knowledge is on the wane in modern times. Increasingly, we are transported by machines rather than our own legs.

Some mystics of the Buddhist tradition practice something called "walking meditation," which is closely related to mindfulness, or moving meditation. And there are groups that encourage barefoot hiking as well. And while this may not appeal to some, depending on the condition of one's feet and that of the chosen trail, there are alternatives, such as striding barefoot over moist grass on a summer morning, or (if you are adventurous) sinking your naked feet into wet mud or sand, letting it squish between your toes. I even walk barefoot on the snow, albeit briefly. Barefoot variations on the Way of Walking provide a direct, sensory-rich way to touch the Earth, and be touched by her in return. Skin-to-skin interaction with the Creation can be more than mere physical contact. It can constitute a unique kind of touching, a form of affection between you and the "Thou" of the soil, sand, or grass.

Method

The Way of Walking involves the following steps:

- As always, the more natural the setting, the better.
- Also, the more natural the walking surface, the better. While hiking and nature trails are good, the experience can be enhanced further by following more primitive paths, such as animal trails. Regarding this, the geographically challenged should be cognizant that animal trails, unlike human-made ones, often lead into mazes and gazebo-like intersections that can disorient anyone without a well-tuned sense of direction. Open prairies, fields, and beaches, as well as bushwhacking through a forest, amplify the primeval feel of the experience, although one should always be careful not to inflict damage on an environmentally fragile or sensitive area.
- Unlike some of the other soulful paths employed by nature mystics, this one incorporates a stronger inward focus, although an awareness of one's surroundings is clearly a part of the mix. Focus your senses on what is commonly called the "proprioceptive" experience, meaning attend to the physical sensations of one's body in motion. Experience at the inner perceptual level what it is like to be bipedal, to move as an animal through your environment, your home. And of course, if you are walking barefoot, you will have a powerful tactile experience as well.
- Your outward sensory focus can be directly linked with your felt-animal experience of walking. Attend to the sound and effects of your body moving, perhaps brushing against grasses or crunching over sand,

rocks, leaves, or crusted snow. Be aware of how you become part of the environment, interacting with it directly through the flow of your movement in tandem with the complex, interweaving entities and processes in your midst.

- Through this balanced sensory focus (the inner sensation of walking combined with the outer experience of interacting with the ecosystem), you may enter what could be termed "gestalt consciousness." This is essentially becoming aware, at an experiential rather than cognitive level, of how you and all the other processes and entities in your interactive environment constitute a functional, complimentary web that connects and oscillates in balance. This mode of consciousness is often a precursor to the mystical state called "the oceanic feeling," where one's sense of being a separate, detached self evaporates into communion with the Creation.

- Once you feel at home with the Way of Walking, you can also learn to dance, in a fashion, with a flowing process in your environment. For example, if you are walking by a beach, you can create a harmonious cadence between your steps and the sound of the waves on the shore. There are many venues for following the lead of some continuous, rhythmic sound in nature, such as crickets, rushing water (walking beside a river or stream), waves on the shore, or wind blowing through trees, grasses, or canyons.

Application

The Way of Walking moves well in these circumstances:

- One is having difficulty getting out of one's mind and into one's senses. In this regard, barefoot walking is particularly helpful.
- Worrying, mental time travel, and excessive thinking are interfering with one's capacity to embrace soulfulness.
- One has lost a sense of being an animal, of feeling one's body as a highly evolved, organic entity (sometimes described as feeling numb from the neck down).
- One wants to progress toward the oceanic mode of consciousness, but in a manner that is gradual and retains a physical grounding in so-called everyday, familiar reality.

Chapter 13

The Way of Sound

Those little nimble musicians of the air that warble forth their curious ditties, with which nature hath furnished them to the shame of art.
—Izaak Walton

For you shall go out in joy, and be led forth in peace;
the mountains and the hills before you shall break forth into singing,
and all the trees of the field shall clap their hands.
—Isaiah 55:12

Most of us are blessed by the gift of hearing.

Even those who are not, such as my older brother, can feel sound, which is why deaf folks sometimes love loud, concussive music. They can take to the dance floor and feel the rhythm through their feet. Which tells us a lot about what sound truly is.

By physical definition, sound is a moving wave that is an oscillation of pressure transmitted through a solid, liquid, or gas. That word—oscillation—tells the better part of the story of hearing. Sound oscillates at certain frequencies, some of which human ears can detect (feel actually) and some that are beyond our range (think dog whistles). How do we detect sounds? Inside our ears there are tiny hairs called cilia that are sensitive to the vibrations associated with certain sounds. Once stimulated, cilia transmit information to the auditory nerve, which then carries it to the brain. Neurologists will argue that we don't actually hear with our ears, but with our brains. Either way, hearing is a salient example of how the boundaries of apparent separation between ourselves and the rest of nature are porous, to say the least. We have the wondrous capacity to detect formless, invisible energy (sound), transform it from tactile movement (of those ear hairs) into electrical energy (transmitted along the auditory nerve) and, finally, into electrochemical information contained in neurotransmitters and neurons, which we utilize to support higher brain functions, such as reasoning, decision-making, and deduction. If that isn't a miracle, then night does not follow day.

Now, in order to travel, sound needs a medium; in this world, that is either a solid (think dance floor), a liquid (think of whales calling to each other), or a gas (think of the space between you and your speakers). In the vacuum of space, we can't hear. So it seems that sound is a property of those planets and moons that possess some manner of atmosphere or liquid sufficient to convey those good vibrations.

And good vibrations were exactly what Marie required. After decades in the C suites of several major corporations and at the pinnacle of her highly successful business career, she began to feel frozen inside, as if her spirit had rusted and then just seized up.

"Kind of like the Tin Man," I suggested, and she agreed.

In every aspect of her person—the emotional, cognitive, interpersonal, spiritual, and physical—she had become rigid, mechanical, and humorless. When she began to question whether she still had the capacity to show her feelings at all, it put such a scare in her that she found her way to me.

"Tin Man, eh? Does that mean I'm clinically depressed?" she asked me.

"It means you need to get your flexibility and spontaneity back," I replied.

On our first hike into the Kettle Moraine State Forest in Wisconsin, I chose a windy day, and we got a wild one. It was autumn and a cold front had just blasted through the upper Midwest, leaving us in blustery 25 knot gusts under an overcast sky. Perfect. I led Marie to a large stand of towering pines. The ground around these majestic sentinels was soft and parched; essentially a bed-like mat of dried pine needles. I pulled a ground cloth from my fanny pack, spread it on the ground under a particularly robust tree, and invited Marie to sit or lay there while I wandered off for a time. Before leaving, I reminded her of what we'd discussed earlier—that all she needed to do was focus on the sounds around her. And that whenever she found her mind pecking away at her awareness with thinking, she should imagine those thoughts turning into static and being absorbed by the cacophony of sounds in her midst.

I returned about thirty minutes later, although I'd actually positioned myself so that I could observe Marie from a distance. To me, it was a safety issue, and being fairly good at concealing myself in the wild, I was confident I would not intrude on her experience. Of course, I will never know what she heard, but I do know what was coming into my ears—a crescendo of wind surfing through the forest canopy, ebbing and flowing like waves crashing ashore. Occasionally, this harmonic flow was punctuated by two trees rubbing together as they swayed, emitting a creaky squawk. It was hypnotizing, and while I watched her lying prone on the ground, I found myself slipping into my own reverie. Sometime later, I was stirred by the sight of Marie lifting her arms skyward, moving them in slow circles, and then in a rhythmic but flailing way, as if she were conducting a symphony.

When I arrived by her side, Marie was still on her back, eyes closed, tears streaming down her cheeks, and a bittersweet smile on her face. She felt my presence.

"It's . . . it's just so beautiful," she half-whispered.

"It's the Creator's music," I suggested.

And of course, all human music has its origins in the sounds of nature. When we listen soulfully to the owl's eerie call, the brook's babble, the cymbal crash of thunder, or the lilting lullaby of crickets, we hear the voice of the Creator. We listen quietly and with rapt attention to the wisdom being "spoken" to us by a power and intelligence far, far greater than our own.

The Way of Sound, like that of wind and water, is a doorway to what New Age devotees and super athletes call "flow." Sound is flowing energy. When we immerse ourselves in this river of oscillating waves, it massages our spirit, helping to loosen the spiritual rust and corrosion precipitated by cynicism and self-objectification. Which is precisely what Marie needed.

What's more, the Way of Sound is particularly helpful for those aspiring nature mystics who struggle with the process of being found. Even those who come away unfulfilled when seeking to be found by a place, stone, tree, or other nature focus, often find this approach easier when it comes to the realm of natural sounds. All that is required is to visit a location where the sounds of nature are not loudly interrupted or drowned out by human noise. Even an urban or suburban park can work in this regard, provided nature is the dominant sound emitter in the area.

Research shows that music can have a profound influence on human emotions and is one of the most rapid and powerful means for changing states of consciousness. Also, repetitive music that is rhythmic has the capacity to induce trance states and other forms of altered consciousness, a fact not lost on earlier tribal cultures where shamans used it for this specific purpose. Anthropologists speculate that the first music created by humans was probably vocal, perhaps followed by rhythmic sounds from hitting stones together, or crude drumming. While in dispute, some date the first musical instrument (a crude flute) to about 25,000 years ago, while others insist that some could have appeared much earlier. Evolutionary biologists speculate that ancient humans probably first created music that mimicked sounds from nature, particularly birdcalls.

Now, while we commonly associate music with humans, nature has its own wide array of musicians, instruments, and songs. Many other creatures generate their own musical sounds, including birds, whales, frogs, crickets, wolves, chipmunks . . . the list is extensive. Like human music, that of other animate life forms is used for communication, but it is also likely that, as we do, other creatures sing out for the sheer enjoyment of creating sound. And of course, other entities and processes in the natural world generate their own music. Waves lapping against a shore, wind rushing through prairie grass, thunder echoing across a landscape, sand swirling over dunes, ice expanding and cracking, leaves dancing in a breeze—the repertoire is diverse and expansive.

And like human music, the Creator's tunes can have a profound influence on our moods and consciousness. Many of us have paused, spellbound, to take in the melodic calls of birds, the calming refrains of waterfalls, the whirring hums of dragon flies, the innervating rumbles of distant storms, or the primal cries of wolves, elk, or hawks, to name a few. When we tune our ears and awareness to these sounds, we hear the music of Creation itself, drawing us toward our spiritual home.

Method

The Way of Sound involves the following:

- Visiting a natural area where nature sounds dominate over human ones.
- Quieting one's self, including the inner chatter of thinking, in order to be receptive to nature's music (consider utilizing the "releasing" ritual in the Way of Wind).
- Most often, it helps to stand, sit, or lay in one place, remaining quiet and unobtrusive for a period of time. When we silently blend in with the environment, more creatures will appear and sally forth with their calls and singing.
- When nature's music arises, simply tune in soulfully, allowing the sounds to fully occupy one's consciousness.

Applications

The Way of Sound carries well in these situations:

- You feel mentally or emotionally rigid, burned out, or stifled.
- You are highly sensitive to sound, meaning it is one of your intrinsic pathways for altering mood and consciousness.

- You are having difficulty with the process of being found by entities and processes in nature. Sounds come to us in a more direct and obvious way.
- Your spirits need lifting.

CHAPTER 14

The Dark Side

Don't underestimate the power of the dark side.

—Darth Vader

In nature there are neither rewards nor punishments—there are consequences.

—Robert Green Ingersoll

It was January 18, so my feet landed with hard, muted thuds on the unforgiving, frozen turf of a Wisconsin prairie.

The wind blew strong and bitterly cold from the east, gusting in advance of an approaching arctic front swooping down from Canada. The dry, brittle grasses bent close to the ground, lashing wildly before the frigid tempest. A layer of steel-gray cirrostratus streamed across the sky, turning the sun into an opaque, fuzzy orb of diffuse and muted light.

Holding close to the edge of a nearby forest as a buffer to the wind, I paused to survey the area, turning slowly in a circle, taking time for my eyes and ears to absorb the environs. Save for the dull red of some dogwood, all was white, grey, black, and washed out brown. Not a smidgen of green was anywhere to be seen. It was, as we say, the dead of winter.

If you enjoy going off-trail and don't mind cold and the absence of vibrant color, winter is a prime time to hike the natural areas of the northern states, like my native Wisconsin. The thick underbrush, impenetrable during spring and summer, can be successfully navigated, albeit with some effort and attention to thorns. Except for fast running streams, the wetlands are frozen and can be traversed rather than avoided. There are no bugs and few people, providing a solitary interlude from two of the most common interruptions one experiences while in a natural setting.

Plodding through a large grassy bog encircled by stands of oak, poplar, and pine, I paused to warm my hands with my breath. Given the opportunity, the bitter cold would rapidly drain the life from my body. To avoid this unhappy outcome, I had adorned my frame with layers of warm clothing, thick gloves, a wool hat, insulated boots, and an outer wind-breaking parka with a hood. Only a small slip of skin around my eyes was exposed to the frigid air. Looking at the landscape of sleeping trees, dry grasses, and bare bushes, I contemplated how the vibrant, active life forces previously visible in these plants had retreated far inside their bark and roots, much as I had encased my own élan vital in sheaths of wool and synthetic insulation.

It brought to mind an autumn backpacking foray of mine into the higher reaches of Glacier Peaks Wilderness in northern Washington State, not far from the Canadian border. Each evening, as the sun disappeared behind the craggy spires, a cold wind swept down from the high crests, rattling our small tents. Despite all the layers of clothing and the high tech sleeping bags, my three companions and I could not stave off the unwavering chill. The nights on this weeklong venture were long and cold, and one had the unnerving sense of being close to an edge, a place where nature has not just ceased to be friendly but has become downright adversarial. The margins for error are thin. A sleeping bag not quite suitable for the subarctic nights, an accidental fall while crossing an ice-encrusted creek, the failure to properly calculate the amount of necessary calories to fuel the body's metabolic furnace, or an unexpected, early blast of winter weather . . . any one of these missteps or twists of fate could rapidly place a person in mortal danger.

In such circumstances, and many others of a similar kind, one is left with one immutable conclusion. Nature, this incredible and mysterious manifestation of a nascent spiritual presence, is abjectly indifferent to the existence of individual creatures, planets, or stars.

If you venture into its realm without proper preparation or knowledge, removing yourself from the safety net of civilization, it will not make allowances for your miscalculations or folly. As Einstein noted, "The universe is a friendly but not always safe place." Meaning that the cosmos is an expression of something profound and intelligent and creative, but this implicit force is not functioning for the sole or primary benefit of humans, particularly entitlement-laden ones. At least from the egocentric perspective of human needs and wants, nature is not without its dark side.

When face-to-face with nature's harsh indifference, staying healthy and alive requires attending to the necessities of survival. Nature won't do that for you. And while, through our technologies, we have insulated ourselves from many of the natural dangers faced by our ancestors, they remain part of the Creation. The universe was not built for our convenience.

This stark and unforgiving fact is at the core of the human predilection for separating God from nature, for regarding one as numinous and sacred and the other as secular and profane. Those who insist on envisioning their deity as benevolent and all loving have difficulty perceiving the natural realm, which is clearly both evil and good (from the human vantage point), as an expression of the divine. Arguably, the concepts of the devil and demonic forces probably emerged, in no small part, from the need to resolve the paradox of believing in a benevolent God that created a not-always-benevolent cosmos. Western philosophers and theologians largely concluded that God is on our side but nature is not.

It is, after all, perplexing to see the creative power of nature manifested in a swarm of killer bees attacking a child, a flash flood sweeping away a village, or an influenza pandemic ravaging the global community. How is one to recognize, let alone honor, the spiritual in nature when the dark and destructive forces of the cosmos are wreaking havoc in one's life? The assertion that the sacred is immanent in the natural world would likely prove unconvincing to the dinosaurs or the other 99 percent of the Earth's species that have disappeared down the one-way abyss of extinction. This lofty concept would have seemed absurd to the creatures inhabiting Earth between 850 to 635 million years ago during the Cryogenian Period, which included the mother of all ice ages. During that frigid era, the planet probably came as close as it ever has to freezing over entirely (some scientists believe it did), leaving the Earth's inhabitants only a few pockets of warmth, such as deep ocean hydrothermal vents, perhaps the original wombs of animate life.

And to bring it closer to home, it is important to remember that our species came close to joining the also-rans. Evolutionary biologists studying the human genome tell us that at some point in our past (estimated at about 70,000 years ago) for reasons not entirely clear our species came very close to disappearing. According to Bernard Wood, Professor of Human Origins at George Washington University, "The evidence would suggest that we came within a cigarette paper's thickness of becoming extinct." The culprit may have been a kind of nuclear winter caused by excessive volcanic activity, virulent disease, or some other environmental catastrophe. Regardless, we came that close to going out forever. What's more, if this near-extinction event was volcanic in nature, geologists predict that a similar global catastrophe of this type and magnitude is all but certain somewhere in our future.

And we are to regard the Creation as sacred?

If there is something awry in all this, it is more likely our way of thinking about nature than it is nature itself. Like earlier humans who insisted that the

Earth was the center of the universe, many of us regard our species as the ultimate expression and purpose of cosmic evolution. It is this very attitude (that humans are the nexus of existence) that underpins the widespread notion that we can do whatever we please with the Earth, its resources, and our fellow creatures.

When the religions based on Abraham (Judaism, Christianity, and Islam) came into being, the proclivity for dividing the world into good and evil took on new theological enthusiasm. Because humans had long struggled with natural forces in order to survive, there was an innate tendency to elevate the divine above the physical universe—a realm that, after all, had the capacity to inflict great suffering and deprivation upon people. If the Almighty was all good, all-knowing, and infinitely compassionate, then surely It could not be within the natural world but, rather, had to be above it—transcendent, pure, and removed. Separating God from the Creation left nature in a one-down posture. People began to equate evil with the destructive forces of nature, at least in part. Hell was believed to be deep inside the Earth itself, while heaven was above it all.

When monotheistic religions began to intellectually separate the sacred from the Creation, then earlier Earth-based beliefs (such as Wicca and Shamanism) were often demonized. They were labeled as "pagan" and in cahoots with the devil. This bias was a key rationalization used by European explorers and settlers to denigrate, steal from, and murder native peoples throughout the world during the Age of Discovery. It is more than sobering to realize that the genocide and cultural persecution of Native Americans, most of who lived in intimate dialogue and harmony with the natural realm, was justified in the name of religious and secular "truths" that implicitly rejected their humanity because of their so-called pagan beliefs.

Historically, the denigration of nature-based spirituality by Western civilization began in earnest during the Black Death (i.e., bubonic plague) that ravaged Europe during the fourteenth century, reducing the population by as much as one to two-thirds. Tribal groups and scattered agricultural communities who practiced various kinds of shamanistic ceremonies and worshiped nature deities rather than "one true god" became scapegoats for political and religious leaders who wanted to blame the epidemic on anyone or anything other than themselves. Believing, as most did, that an all-loving deity would not inflict such carnage on people without just cause, the majority went looking for a minority who must have offended their god. Hence, the term "pagan" was born, referring to someone who either has no recognized religion or follows a polytheistic (many gods) or pantheistic (one god in all things) faith. This us-versus-them posture toward so-called Paganism laid the attitudinal groundwork for much of the cultural genocide perpetrated against Native Americans, and, in various guises, it continues to this day.

The way so-called pagan religions came to terms with nature's dark side was by carving out places in their theologies for the "dark spirits." These people worshipped or recognized deities (their symbols for the forces of nature) that were both benevolent and destructive. Accepting the dark side as part of their view of life proved their undoing. "Naturism," like racism and sexism, is alive to this day, emerging in a plethora of social and religious practices, from the notion that "God's chosen people" have total dominion over nature to the insidious and widespread attitude that the Earth is not a living, sacred entity but simply a ball of rock and resources that we may voraciously and heedlessly plunder.

To call us an elitist species puffed up with hubris is putting it lightly. But should we accept it, the dark side of nature offers an antidote in this regard.

When we are exposed to nature's power and, at times, its fury, or when we intentionally place ourselves in close contact with the natural world without benefit of our usual technology and creature comforts, then we can begin to realize that humans are not the center of the universe. While some find this disturbing and while the dark side of the Creation can clearly be terrifying, there is a vital perspective to be gained in such circumstances.

Nature, including those aspects of it that seem adversarial toward human life and limb, helps us discover our legitimate place in the natural order, that of one entity which, while blessed with its own unique talents, is simply one among many. The nature mystic embraces the humility that many religions admonish us to feel and practice if we truly aspire to a spiritual life. One cannot be genuinely humble if one embraces the way of the ego, the me-myself-and-I mentality that fuels our lack of stewardship toward the Earth and our incivility toward each other. In the presence of the natural realm, be that in a moment of awe and joy or one of cowering terror, we find our place in the greater reality. And we sometimes find a unity with one another that otherwise eludes us. Consider, for example, how often we discard our petty differences and pull together when beset by natural disasters. As the alien visitor (played by Jeff Bridges) in the movie *Starman* said in describing our species, "You are at your best when things are at their worst."

Immersed as many of us are in our creature comforts and technologically induced delusions of superiority, large numbers of us have become what I call "pronoids," roughly the opposite of a paranoid. Colloquially speaking, a paranoid is someone who believes the universe is a conspiracy against him or her. In contrast, a pronoid is someone who believes the universe is a conspiracy in her or his favor. The way of the nature mystic is not for pronoids. Rather, it is for those who are sufficiently spiritually evolved (or willing to be) that they can accept their minor role in an immense and incredibly long cosmic story. It is for people who have grown beyond the childishly egocentric attitude that their individual importance can somehow trump the course of cosmic evolution in their favor.

If we are to hear, in whatever small way, the expressions of the scared within the Creation, then we must listen to all its sounds, the beautiful and repulsive, the creative and destructive, the numinous and the bleak.

The many in the one.

CHAPTER 15

The Way of Storms

Wonders are many, and none is more wonderful than the power that crosses the white sea, driven by the stormy wind, making a path under surges that threaten to engulf him . . .

—Sophocles

Nature has no mercy at all. Nature says, "I'm going to snow. If you have on a bikini and no snowshoes, that's tough. I am going to snow anyway."

—Maya Angelou

Storms.

They come to us from what we perceive as the dark side of nature wherein reside the menacing and indifferent forces that randomly bedevil our efforts to make a tidy world. While some of us may revel in the thunder's crack, the wind's roar, the gale's pounding waves, or the blizzard's frigid grasp, many more grumble in discontent or cower in dread. All that we have to learn from tempests, some would assert, is how to stay out of their way. After all, at a minimum, storms can be discomforting and disruptive and, at a maximum, they lay waste to people and places, at times on a massive scale.

This evening, as I write this chapter, my community in Wisconsin is being ravaged by a 300 mile long, 40 mile wide ramrod of storms. In the current stillness, lightning blazes around us, striking the Earth with deafening cracks, followed by ultralow, rumbling thunder from all directions. The heavens have opened and we are deluged, as storm cell after cell moves slowly overhead, west to east. On the fringes of this elongated and intense system, there are wildly swirling gale force winds and multiple tornadoes hopscotching from farm to town. The weather radio sounds repeated alarms, and through the relentless roar of the rain, the warning siren blares, rotating away and then back again. A true tempest.

But what are storms actually? Fundamentally, a storm is a perturbation of wind, air pressure, heat energy, and water vapor. The meteorological term for a storm is a "cyclone," which is basically an area of low atmospheric pressure encircled by winds that spiral inward, not unlike water being sucked down a drain. In the middle latitudes of Earth's northern hemisphere, cyclones travel primarily from west to east and produce rain events, thunderstorms, tornadoes, winter storms, and blizzards. The same is true in similar latitudes of the southern hemisphere, except they traverse largely east to west, depending on prevailing winds. In the tropics, cyclones produce hurricanes and typhoons, often the largest maelstroms, although some winter storms in the middle latitudes can be immense as well. Whereas tornadoes and thunderheads usually affect limited geographic areas for short spans of time, tropical storms, hurricanes, dust storms, and massive blizzards can pummel entire continents and last for weeks.

Regardless of how destructive storms may be to those who experience them at their worst, they are vital to maintaining the Earth's heat balance, another critical variable in sustaining organic life forms. Latent heat energy builds up in the air, threatening to disrupt atmospheric homeostasis. Storms come to the system's rescue. A hurricane, for instance, releases heat at a rate of 50 to 200 trillion watts, roughly the equivalent of a 20 megaton nuclear device exploding every few seconds. While thunderstorms, winter storms, and tornadoes are less robust, collectively they are critical in keeping global temperatures in a benign range, not to mention for the transfer of water vapor and precipitation from liquid surfaces (mostly oceans) to landmasses. About 40,000 thunderstorms pummel the planet each day, and from them collectively, lightning crackles at a rate of approximately 100 bolts each second. Each of those bolts, traveling at about 270,000 miles per hour, heats the surrounding air to a temperature considerably hotter than the surface of the sun.

All of which is to say that storms, like them or not, are a vital part of the web of life.

But there is more to a storm than simply an impressive and sometimes adverse expression of concentrated atmospheric energy. Like all entities in the natural world, storms are living illustrations of the ingenious power and majesty of the Creation. Their scientific admirers sometimes describe them as "orderly chaos," meaning that while their effects are often wild and unpredictable, they are fueled by self-sustaining and self-regulating forces that support longer-term environmental equilibrium. What's more, storms demonstrate the awesome and sometimes terrifying beauty of what we have called the "dark side" of nature. And as such, they fascinate and even mesmerize us.

As a teenager, I recall cowering in a rural roadside ditch with a mix of terror and fascination as a tornado thundered through a nearby field of corn. Frightened for my life, I still could not help but peer up over the grassy rise to behold what clearly seemed the wrath of God. As a Great Lakes sailor, I have had similar moments when ensnared in the clutches of a gale, tossed about on a sizable boat made insignificant by towering waves, blinding spindrift, and the screeching of wind in rigging. Many of us can recall comparable moments when at the mercy of storms. They brand themselves on our psyches, not simply because of their drama and intensity, but also because during these events we came soul-to-soul with the Creator's awesome power. At once frightened for our safety, we are simultaneously swooning in a kind of spiritual rapture. One's ego, no matter how puffed up and confident under normal circumstances, sits huddled and quaking in the corner of one's persona. Only the soul can manage to rear its head, turn haltingly to the tempest, and dare to look its maker in the eye.

Storms bring us to the illusive perceptual boundary that artificially separates what we call matter from what we term energy. While we distinguish these two properties (matter and energy) in our thinking and, consequently, our perception, they are a unified aspect of the quantum field that innervates the entire Creation. As nature author Bill Bryson puts it, "Energy is liberated matter; matter is energy waiting to happen." In every so-called material thing, including a cumulonimbus cloud (or thunderhead), a hailstone, or a raindrop, there is an incredible amount of latent energy. Consider your own body, which you probably experience as a hunk of matter rather than a crackling collection of relatively stable energy. If you are of average size, you harbor enough potential energy to explode with the power of over thirty hydrogen bombs. I hope you won't, of course, not only for your own sake but because this would be a particularly destructive demonstration of spontaneous combustion. Nonetheless, a storm is an expression of the tidal interplay between perceived matter (water vapor, atmospheric gases, precipitation, etc.) and perceived energy (wind, lightning, pressure gradients, etc.). Within it, the dance of matter and energy is clearly evident, powerful, and ever changing.

Although many are willing to embrace soulfulness only under copasetic conditions, in contrast, more than a few nature mystics welcome the storm as gladly as the balmy day, or even more. By immersing themselves in its sound and fury, they experience an intensity of interaction with the Creation that often feels more immediate and available than that during the relative serenity of more benign weather. Most of us, mystical or not, have experienced that palpable sense of being more alive during and after contact with the so-called natural elements. Simply walk in the rain, allowing it to soak you through, and you will feel a vibrancy in your senses that may otherwise be elusive. Venture out in a swirling wind, plunge through drifting snow, stand next to crashing surf pummeling the shore—and you will likely notice how the make-believe of thinking dissipates and is replaced by the body-felt awareness of a creature fully communing with its physical environment. Within such soulful dialogue, the power of the Creation bursts forth from the amorphous "soup" of matter and energy.

Lest such reverie seem too seductive, remember that a storm is the dark side, and it can be lethally unforgiving. Like the pilgrim daring to look up into the face of God, the nature mystic who plunges into I-Thou interaction with the Creation through the door of the storm is in harm's way. As a youngster, it was my imprudent custom to rush out to the open space of my backyard to greet squall lines as they charged across the Illinois landscape. I reveled in standing there, head up, eyes wide, arms open, exposing my person and soul to the indifferent fury of wind, rain, and lightning. I was not smart, just lucky. There are safer ways to interact with storms, as we shall see.

Method

While it may be obvious to those who are highly experienced in the wild and with adverse weather conditions, the Way of Storms should be approached *very* carefully. Here are some of the more benign venues for doing so:

- A rainstorm absent lightning (thunder being an obvious indicator that lightning is present) is a relatively safe context for immersion in the Way of Storms. If the rain is excessive, then one should avoid creeks, ditches, and riverbeds that might flash flood, as well as low-lying areas where deeper pools of water may collect or create dangerously porous footing. Be mindful that certain surfaces, such as mud without vegetation, specific types of clay (such as adobe), and peat, or other permeable materials can be hazardous during heavy rain, both in terms of falling and becoming trapped in muck.

- Snowstorms, if not extreme, are also comparatively harmless, again provided one is properly clothed and, if not, close to warm shelter. Recognize that blizzards, which combine high winds, deadly cold, and heavy and often blinding snow, are an exception. It is possible to become lost in a blizzard by venturing even short distances (a few feet) away from shelter. Also, slogging through deep snow requires that one be in excellent physical shape and without heart or lung ailments. When immersed in the fury of a winter storm, hypothermia is a definite and potentially deadly threat unless one is properly attired and knowledgeable about cold weather survival.

- Provided they are not extreme, windstorms are an excellent and generally safe venue for pursuing the Way of Storms. Again, be prudent about the intensity of the wind, which becomes problematic once at gale force—roughly 40 mph or greater. And make certain your immediate environment does not have any dangerous objects that, once made airborne, could become potentially lethal projectiles. Finally, don't stand under a tall tree, for instance, as large branches can come down without warning. Beyond that, opening your body and soul to an onrushing wind is both healing and exhilarating.

- In general, any storm that includes lightning, very high winds, tornadoes, flooding, large hail, extreme cold, deadly wind chill, storm surges (as in hurricanes), blinding snow, and similar life or limb-threatening characteristics is not to be trifled with. Be smart and be safe.

- Having perhaps irritated you with caveats and cautions, the Way of Storms remains an awe-inspiring and powerful path for experiencing the Creation. Being in a storm does not require as much conscious effort to employ soulfulness, as the environment tends to take one's senses and consciousness hostage rather than merely inviting them inside. Many find that the intensity of the Way of Storms facilitates the I-Thou interaction that may elude them in more serene circumstances.

Application

The Way of Storms is particularly helpful when:

- You have had difficulty embracing soulfulness in other natural venues.
- Thinking and "aboutism" have proven particularly difficult to dislodge from your consciousness.
- You are inclined, by temperament, to higher amplitude events as ways of transporting your consciousness away from the confines of the ego and its cognitive fiefdom and toward a sense of experiential oneness with the Creation.
- You have fallen prey to excessive pride, self-absorption, or egotism. Hey, it happens to most of us, including yours truly.
- A strong and persistent longing to "see God" has taken hold of your soul.

CHAPTER 16

The Way of Night

Night, the beloved. Night, when words fade and things come alive. When the destructive analysis of day is done, and all that is truly important becomes whole and sound again. When man reassembles his fragmentary self and grows with the calm of a tree.

—Antoine De Saint-Exupery

Darkness has long been a source of fear or, at least, wariness in our species. When our ancestors succeeded in pushing back the night with the mastery of fire and, later, electricity, we insulated ourselves from dangers that skulked around us unseen. The initial edge that other carnivores enjoyed in preying on our kind, often nocturnally, slowly began to shift in our direction. But species memory is strong and even in this modern epoch, many of us fear the night. As a young child, any foray into the shadowy abyss of my basement set my heart to flutter and my mind to flights of nightmarish fantasy. Even as adults, many would find being encircled by darkness in the woods while alone at night a near-breathless ordeal.

On my backpacking excursions, I sometimes rise from sleep, venture from my tent into the blackness, and stand for a time, engulfed by a unique blindness that one suffers despite having one's eyes wide open. Many people don't truly comprehend the reality behind the phrase, "I couldn't see my hand in front of my face." Those who do realize how night, somewhat like storms, humbles the ego, impressing it with its vulnerabilities and smallness. Perhaps darkness is too akin to what we imagine about death, the possibility of an endless night. Or maybe it simply disarms us, transporting us back in time to when hominids were rendered utterly vulnerable by their inability to see while simultaneously being quite visible to those creatures that would eat them.

But night is not all about fear. It is also about both cloister and mystery.

In darkness we can find a measure of protection, of insulation from the world, from its demands and inspections and judgments. We become, in some sense, invisible and unknown. We experience, at an intuitive level, a kind of forgetting of the social, public persona that we march out each day to spin and flip in the interpersonal circus of human affairs. Within the night, our lives can become, even if briefly, more private and more singularly our own. Even a nighttime stroll about one's neighborhood, be it sufficiently quiet and relatively dark, can evoke this feeling of being cloaked in the protective mantle of the shadows.

In the animal world, night is a very active time. Nocturnal creatures, like owls, bats, fireflies, catfish, tarantulas, raccoons, some foxes, lemurs, and many others, take advantage of the cloak of darkness to go about the business of survival. Unlike humans, these organisms have adapted to the dark in impressive ways. Owls, for example, have superior night vision that allows them to hunt in conditions where we'd be hard-pressed to take a stroll without doing a dirt dive. Meaning that nighttime is not our usual element. In fact, until our forebears began to push back the darkness with fire, torches, lanterns, and, most recently, electric lighting, we humans were quite helpless when out and about at night. This species memory remains with us, and most people find the dark a bit unnerving, if not outright frightening. For the nature mystic, however, the darkness while outdoors is a venue for both confronting one's fears and for experiencing the mysterious within the unseen, the latter being a hallmark of mysticism. In an interesting fashion, these two elements—fear and mystery—often go together.

And that's what Nathan realized, albeit subconsciously, when he sought my guidance. A twenty-something grad student in biology, he was an aspiring nature mystic who, as a child, had felt a strong spiritual bond with the natural world. However, in recent years, this heartfelt connection had waned, leaving him in a "just clouds" frame of mind.

"When I was a kid, nature was full of mystery for me, but now it seems just kind of there, like a big, intricate machine," he shared with me.

His lament evoked memories from my childhood when, one night, I awakened fully to the sacred power within the Creation.

My family and I were driving somewhere in western Nebraska, Dad at the wheel, the rest of the clan curled up in various contorted positions in our '58 Chevy wagon, trying to catch a few winks as we sped through the night toward Colorado. The hum of the tires on the asphalt had lulled me into a fitful sleep, but when the car rattled over some ruts, I was jostled back toward waking consciousness. In a blur, I peered up at Dad, his face faintly illuminated by the dashboard lights.

It was 1959, and we were on a cross-country foray from Illinois to Denver to visit relatives. While that may not sound like much of a hike in the twenty-first century, it was a considerable haul back then. Our journey required that we travel two-lane highways the entire route (there were few interstates at the time), and on the Great Plains one had to carefully plan for gas stops or else pay the price in lost time, shoe leather, and consternation. Also, there were no fast food establishments, so provisions (homemade sandwiches, fruit, soft drinks, chips, and candy bars) were usually carted along in a cooler and picnic baskets. Our gas-guzzling eight-cylinder was without air-conditioning, cruise control, power windows, or other take-it-for-granted conveniences of modern transport, so the wear and tear on the occupants, particularly in the summer heat, was considerable. Hence driving through the night.

Alternately dozing and stirring, I periodically peered out the window and up at the big sky that is characteristic of the Great Plains. Away from city lights, one could glimpse a spectacular swath of stars in a thick ribbon slicing across the zenith of the firmament. Separating the pinpoints of distinct stars and the frothy band of the Milky Way was an abyss of darkness without horizon or dimension.

A one point, we pulled into a wayside surrounded by towering cottonwoods. As the others went in search of privies, I felt something beckoning to me, but without a voice. For reasons I don't quite understand, I staggered off into the darkness until I stumbled and groped my way to the top of a nearby knoll, attracted by a sense of mystery and wonder, but for what, I knew not. Standing in the blackness, I stopped and cocked my head all the way back, my body slowly turning as I strained to drink in the entire dome of the visible universe. Wherever I cast my gaze, the majesty and mystery floated overhead, silent and sentinel, unwavering.

But then something drew my eyes back toward terra firma, fixing them on the far horizon where a faint glow in the sky silhouetted a distant butte. I didn't realize it at that moment, but the Earth was rotating toward the Moon, which was soon to "rise," and its reflective light was gradually illuminating the sky, pushing back the edge of the darkness.

It was then that I felt it.

Describing the ineffable is always risky business. Each of us has experienced moments in our lives that will not submit to words, which refuse to be captured in the nets of our intellects. Even when in the presence of a wise and affirming friend, one struggles and sometimes fails to convey an experience that resonated so deeply and essentially in one's soul. It is a bit akin to trying to describe a visual scene with terminology. As the adage goes, a picture is worth a thousand words, but a thousand words may not be worth a picture. Such is the case even more so when the "picture" is a dark door that opens to the miracle of existence.

Perhaps all I can say is that something on or around or perhaps within that gradually brightening horizon "spoke" to me. And when it did, all the circumstantial accoutrements of my situation in space and time (being my named persona at a Nebraska rest stop with my family in the dead of night) slipped away. There I stood, eyes wide, mind quieted, and spirit rising, all ears to the silent language that was echoing through my soul.

And quite abruptly, but without visible fanfare, time was no more. I was no place and yet everywhere. Indeed, even the sense of "I" as distinct and different from all else vanished like a bubble popping in the air. Within this rapture, I heard, but not a voice; I saw, but not a vision; I touched, but not a thing.

The Creation.

I don't know how long I was not there, so to speak. My sister's voice carried through the stillness, and her irritated admonitions began registering in my ears. I yelled back and then returned to the parking area. They had been calling for me, my sister scolded, and what was the matter with me anyway? Speechless and unresisting, I staggered as she pulled me toward the car. Later, listening to my family members, it was explained that I must have fallen asleep on my feet, or was at least too "out of it" to know what I was doing. I made no protest. The numinous wake left over from Creation's open door was still swirling about me, even as it gradually abated.

For days after, no matter where I was, who with, or what doing, I felt myself drifting back to that moment of dark immersion. In fact, the ripples from that fleeting contact continue to reverberate in my being to this day, almost five decades later; so much so that, each time I go into the night, I sense it. In the darkness, I can revisit that interlude when the spiritual essence implicit in nature allowed me to consciously live, however briefly, in its grace.

So I understood Nathan's need.

"When you think of the mysterious, what comes to mind?" I asked him.

"Night," he said without hesitation, and I asked, "Why?"

"I'm not exactly sure," he answered. "That's just the first thought that came to me."

"I trust that," I told him. "So let's go with the Way of Night."

At home in the natural world during the day, Nathan was not comfortable outdoors in the dark, at least not without some means of illumination. As for taking what I call a "night hike," he never had, but he was a game guy and, after a bit of contemplation, agreed to give it a try. I suggested a trail in the wilds of Michigan's Upper Peninsula, where we both resided at that time, and we conducted a day hike there to familiarize him with the lay of the land. The proposed route was a heavily forested trail that wound through stands of cedar, hemlock, and pine, with occasional openings in wetlands bordered by tamarack, one of a small collection of trees that are deciduous conifers (their "needles" turn yellow and drop in the autumn, just like leaves).

The plan called for Nathan to hike alone into this area on a moonlit night, taking some basic survival gear, as well as a headlamp. For safety, we arranged for him to call me upon his exit, which was to occur during a predetermined window of time. We didn't discuss soulfulness, per se, but I encouraged him to pay attention to any intuitions he had about where to stop and settle into a particular location (being found by place).

"It's all about hearing," he later reported. "I was basically blind without the headlamp on, and even when it was, I couldn't see very far or in my peripheral vision."

By reducing or eliminating visual input, the night compels us to "see" with our ears. On my own night hikes, I frequently stop to listen. Usually, it is so quiet that my own footfalls seem loud and clearly interfere with my ability to hear what is occurring around me. When I am in the act of walking, I make sufficient noise (it doesn't take much) to dissuade other creatures from coming close. But when I take time to stop and be still, the rest of the neighborhood starts to gradually emerge.

"I was in maybe a half mile and decided to stop for a minute, and I was surrounded by this din of frogs just croaking away. Must have been hundreds in that bog," he explained. "The sound was ancient. I felt like some proto-human in the primeval forest."

Even in a dark corner of a city park, being immersed in the night imparts a sense of the primitive. All the visual reminders of our technological ascendancy are nowhere to be seen. One of our species' weak points—poor night vision—becomes a substantial liability, and being bipedal offers its own set of disadvantages on a trail shrouded in blackness, as falling is a real risk. Combining this with the fact that there are probably nocturnal creatures watching your every move, and the experience becomes one of vulnerability.

"I kept the headlamp off mostly. My night vision got better over time, and the Moon provided some illumination, but only in the open spots. Besides, using the lamp made it easier for whatever was out there to see me," he chuckled.

That's a major part of the vulnerable feeling. Knowing that you can be seen while also recognizing that you can't see what can see you percolates into a desire to flee or hide, or at least keep a low profile. Which is exactly what Nathan did.

"Using the headlamp, I found a big hemlock, and I just sat up against it. It felt better having something to back me up, so to speak, and it let me be real quiet and just blend in," he explained.

Without intending to, Nathan soon found himself in a state of consciousness that I simply call "being the night." Sitting quietly beneath what he later labeled his "guardian angel tree," he allowed the darkness to fully envelope him. He could make out shafts of dim moonlight high in the forest canopy, but at ground level, he couldn't see his hand in front of his face. The chorus of frogs, now a mile or more behind, were all but out of earshot, but some crickets had taken up the beat. Feeling the tree against his back, Nathan felt the boundary between his sense of self and the larger Creation become increasingly porous.

"It sounds weird, but everything was just black. The forest, the tree behind me, my own body . . . everything. And then I just became the night. I don't know how else to say it," he told me, his eyes staring off diffusely.

"And what did the night leave with you?" I asked.

Nathan smiled warmly, like you would on greeting a long absent, old friend.

"Wonder," he said, looking up at me. "Wonder."

You don't have to stumble about among bears, pumas, and snakes to embrace the Way of Night. Even quiet neighborhoods, parks, or rural settings can convey a taste of the mystery inherent on the dark side of the planet.

Method

The Way of Night involves:

- Determining a safe venue in which to be in the night, always being mindful not to take unnecessary risks or to push beyond one's knowledge or capabilities. In point of fact, it is often safer to be in the darkness in the wild than on some city streets.
- Blending in with the night. While a flashlight or headlamp should be required equipment if you venture far from home or go into unfamiliar locales, standing or sitting in complete or near darkness is often helpful in creating the kind of consciousness I call "being the night."
- For those who are uncomfortable in the dark, choosing a moonlit night is often a good option. Particularly when there is snow cover, moonlight can provide sufficient ambient glow to allow navigating without need of a flashlight. What's more, with its ethereal dance of shadows and muted illumination, moonlit nights can enhance one's sense of mystery and wonder, while reducing anxiety (unless you believe in werewolves, of course).

Application

The Way of Night is helpful when:

- You have lost touch with that childlike sense of wonder and mystery toward the natural world.
- There is a desire to find cloister from the frenzy, noise, and busyness of the day, when life seems to career along at fever pitch.
- You are bedeviled by anxiety or nameless fears. Being in the night is an act of courage and trust that can ameliorate apprehensiveness. However, if your issues in this regard seem severe or debilitating, engaging the guidance of a trained counselor or nature therapist is prudent.

CHAPTER 17

The Way of Clouds

You must not blame me if I do talk to the clouds.
—Henry David Thoreau

For a nature mystic, clouds are a moving metaphor, a visible representation of the underlying process that drives the Creation. In clouds we can witness the emergence of new forms, seemingly out of thin air, as we say. As they manifest, grow, combine, recede, and eventually disappear, these amorphous shapes illustrate the dance of form and energy that characterizes the life force and the creative verve of the cosmos. Soulfully observing clouds, then, exposes the nature mystic to a microcosm representing the Creation itself.

But what are clouds anyway?

They are both simple and elegant. Clouds are accumulations of tiny droplets of water, ice, and particulate matter (think dust) that are so light they can float in the air. Now, air contains water in the form of vapor which, when near the ground, is largely invisible. But when air rises up in the atmosphere, it usually cools, and cooler air cannot hold as much water vapor as warmer air near the surface, so the vapor condenses into droplets, forming around tiny specks of dust that are floating about. When these tiny droplets collect in the billions, they become a cloud.

Now, clouds are a pivotal player in weather and climate, and not just on Earth. They are found on many planets that have an atmosphere. Jupiter, for example, is famous for its bright bands of fast moving clouds, not to mention the Great Red Spot, which is a hurricane-like tempest that has persisted for at least 400 years and is large enough to swallow three Earths. Closer to home, clouds bring us precipitation and storms, play a part in regulating global temperatures, and constitute the backbone of the varied forms of weather we encounter across the planet, including fog, which is essentially a cloud hugging the ground.

If you've ever plopped down on your back and just watched clouds overhead, you've likely noticed that they are ever changing, sometimes slowly and, on occasion, with breathtaking speed. They can assume a near infinite variety of shapes and hues. It is particularly fascinating to observe a cloud as it comes into being, seemingly out of a clear blue sky. An individual cloud, such as a puffy cumulus, often starts as a tiny sphere of water vapor that, as it grows, slowly emerges from apparent nothingness. Kind of like us and many other life forms and natural processes. We begin as tiny cells that, like the particles of water vapor in a cloud, slowly propagate, take shape, and emerge into the visible universe. And just like those clouds, we eventually come apart, dissipate, and return to the invisible. And herein lies some of the attraction found in the Way of Clouds. By observing them, we see the birth, growth, maturity, degradation, and death that is the modus operandi of the Creation's great recycling process. And we witness a clear manifestation of nature as a creative force.

Which was what Allison needed. A writer, photographer, and thespian, she had long relied on her inner muse to stoke the embers of her creative fires. She regarded her art as a spiritual process, one that placed her in harmony with the larger creative energies coursing through the cosmos.

"When I write or take a photograph, it's all about spirit," she told me. "Without that muse whispering in my ear or showing me that next shot, I'm dead in the water."

And that's where she found herself in the months preceding our initial visit; drifting without benefit of the creative winds that had blown through her soul for so long. This had a deleterious impact not only on her artistic output, but also on her joy, as well as her sense of meaning and purpose. As she put it, this was a "spiritual crisis for me." As such, it required a spiritual response. But when I asked her to be found by something in nature that embodied the creative verve she sought to regain, she came up blank.

"I've tried flowers and waterfalls and bird songs . . . all kinds of stuff. But it all just leaves me flat now," Allison lamented.

"How about clouds?" I asked.

"Clouds? I've never thought of clouds as being a creative force. I mean, they can be pretty and all, but they're just up there," she replied.

"You may want to take another look," I suggested. "But this time, don't just look with your eyes. Look with your heart, your spirit."

So after a bit of coaching on soulfulness, she was ready to seek her muse. Being an amateur meteorologist, I alerted her when the weather would be best for cloud watching. So when a copasetic day arrived, she made her way to a high hill in a nearby state forest, one that was open prairie, affording an unimpeded panorama of the sky. As she reclined on her blanket, gazing up into the heavens, she remembered my admonition: "Don't just look at the clouds. *Be* the clouds."

"I have to tell you," she later reported. "I thought this whole idea was kind of silly, but I was desperate."

And at first, it did indeed feel silly to her. She kept fidgeting, and not just in her limbs. Her thinking mind twitched like a toad, pestering her psyche with all manner of cognitive dissonance, worry, and awkward self-consciousness. Then that thought came to her once more. *Be* the clouds.

"I kept thinking, how the hell am I supposed to be a cloud?" she told me afterward. "But then I remembered my acting."

Allison slipped into an improvisational mode, one she had learned a decade earlier in drama class.

"They had us be all sorts of things . . . chairs, cats, trees. So I figured, what can be so tough about being a cloud?"

Over the next hour or so, Allison became dozens of clouds floating overhead. The sky was adrift in fair weather cumulus, which are puffy cotton ball-type shapes that drift slowly over the landscape. Each is distinct, varying in form, size, and shading. At first, mostly just using her body, she did her best to assume the shape of a particular cloud, all this while still lying on her back. As the cloud morphed, she morphed with it.

"Before long, I didn't have to work at it much. I just really got into it. I mean, those clouds were so beautiful and light and airy. They really put the zap on me," she reported.

Before long, Allison's thinking mind took a hike. She became fully immersed in *being* the clouds, and soon crossed over into a kind of "trance state," as she termed it. After an hour or so, she drifted into a light sleep.

"My muse woke me up," she said. "I was just zoned out there on the ground, and then I heard it. Well, it's not like actual hearing, but it's in your head, you know? And as I woke up, it was giving me an idea for a new article."

Allison was dead in the water no more. She'd been transported away from her creative doldrums by an unlikely I-Thou interaction. Now, she is a person of the clouds.

Method

The Way of Clouds can be followed by:

- Inhabiting a quiet, comfortable location that offers an open view of the sky.

- Choosing a day when clouds are present. They don't have to be any particular type of cloud. Just let your intuition tell you which might be best.
- Assuming a comfortable position for cloud watching, one that won't leave you with a stiff neck. And if you do lay on your back, which most folks prefer, feel free to use a blanket, and be sure to check for any unwanted companions underneath (an anthill, for instance).
- Doing some deep breathing or another relaxation method in order to put a sock in your thinking brain. If you are familiar with meditation, work with your breathing first, eyes closed, and then open your eyes and begin focusing on what is overhead.
- Visually "drink in" the clouds. In particular, it may be interesting to follow a particular one as it progresses across the sky, watching how it transforms under the influence of wind, heat, and time.
- If you are so inclined, "being" one of the clouds, much as Allison did. We will look at that in the Way of Being chapter, which is next.

Application

The Way of Clouds drifts well in these circumstances:

- Your wellspring of creativity has run dry.
- Your mind has become too literal, too concrete. As such, the world feels more like a machine or a thing than a living, creating force.
- You find yourself fearful about or unable to change. Clouds are powerful and engaging symbols of ongoing transformation.
- You would simply enjoy engaging your imagination, to regain some of that childlike "seeing" that is stifled by being too grown up.

CHAPTER 18

The Way of Being

The body is the location of all knowledge. What we "know" comes to us through our senses, throughout contact with physical, earthly experience. That experience invariably shapes what we perceive. Perception is inherently participatory. To the body, the world is not "object." There is no "me" apart from an "other." Everything is animate for the sensing body. Touch a tree and the tree is touching you back.
—Larry Parks Daloz paraphrasing David Abram

In seeking communion with the natural world, nature mystics aspire to a deep level of spiritual rapport I call the Way of Being.

The various practices we have examined, such as soulfulness and being found, are steps toward this form of communion. However, there is another approach that has the potential for even more intimate confluence between a human and another aspect of the Creation. Perhaps the best term to describe it is "blending," a process that seeks to reduce or remove the barriers in one's consciousness that maintain a sense of separation between one's self and that of another entity or process in the natural world. Now, the idea that humans can experience communion with a seemingly totally separate aspect of nature may seem the province of an overactive imagination or even self-delusion, but it actually has a basis in science. Let's briefly consider that.

Until early in the twentieth century, physicists believed in a universe in which objects and processes could be truly separate from and unaffected by one another. It seemed apparent that not all entities and events interacted and that unless they did so by physical means (touch, for example), they had no impact on each other. A mango tree in Vietnam had no influence on a prairie in

Nebraska. An exploding supernova on the far side of the galaxy did not affect our own solar system. However, this "collection of different and unrelated things" view of the universe started unraveling when physicists began to study matter and energy below the atomic level, in the so-called quantum realm. That's when they discovered that the act of observing something, even without touching it, had an influence on that something.

This view got legs in 1927 with the emergence of what is called "the Uncertainty Principle," which was promulgated by Werner Heisenberg, a theoretical physicist. His tenet, which was derived from experiments in quantum physics, asserts that there is no such thing as an objective observer who is entirely separate from what she or he observes. Instead, we are what might be called "participatory observers." Applied to consciousness and human perception, this means that when we interact with something in nature, even if only by direct observation, we influence it. When one beholds a tree, there is no fixed objective reality "out there" which is being studied by another totally separate objective reality (you or me) "in here." Rather, by the very act of observing, we alter and participate in creating an aspect of the phenomenon in question.

By way of illustration, represent yourself by drawing a circle on a piece of paper. Now, draw a second circle that represents the tree you are observing. In the old view, the two circles don't touch. You look at the tree, the tree stands there, and that's that. Now, draw the two circles again but in such a way that they overlap about halfway. The overlapping portion is a kind of "shared space" that is created between you and the tree, a space that exists only by virtue of your interaction with each other. That is the space you experience when soulfully interacting with a tree, or anything else. It is the space the nature mystic seeks to enter through the Way of Being.

Now, our common sense tells us that this is not so, that we can actually be detached, separate observers who refrain from influencing what we scrutinize. But as Heisenberg reminded us, "What we observe is not nature itself, but nature exposed to our method of questioning."

Now most of us understand that by tangibly interacting with a material object or process, we alter it. Consider a brook, for example. Our common sense tells us that if we simply look at the water without entering or touching it, we have not altered it. The water is out there and we are in here, there is a space separating the two and, this gap not having been crossed, they have not directly affected each other. But the Uncertainty Principle suggests we may be wrong about that, at least at the foundational level of existence, which is all about energy. It asserts that by merely observing the water, whether by sight or sound or even just by our presence, we change it. Granted, in order to fully experience the water, one must enter it in some physical or sensory fashion.

However, the Uncertainty Principle tells us that observation (i.e., a euphemism for a form of participatory interaction) creates a shared space with that brook. It is never the same again, nor are we. The so-called observer and that which is seemingly being observed are engaged in an interactive relationship that *creates*, rather than merely records, reality.

Now, this can easily sound like New Age gibberish. If I seek to "observe" a tornado by stepping in harm's way and "participating" in its emerging existence, I will suffer the obvious consequences. We inhabit a world that has rules governing our material condition and survival. Nevertheless, when we drill down to the fundamental building blocks (processes actually) of this seemingly immutable reality of ours, the rules, boundaries, and limitations that look and feel so rock solid at our everyday level of experience start to dissolve. We discover that the sea of existence is not composed of countless individual droplets of water, so to speak, but rather is one continuous and unified happening.

The idea of participatory consciousness, which is key to the Way of Being, is also supported by something called Quantum Entanglement, which Einstein referred to as "spooky action at a distance." Sub-atomic particles (inside of atoms) have an attribute called "spin" (think of a top), and when these particles bind in pairs (i.e., create a shared space), their respective spins move in opposite directions (another "opposites attract" metaphor). Physicists discovered that if you separate these previously connected particles and send one of them far away from its partner and then reverse its spin, the particle that is left behind instantaneously reverses its spin as well. In other words, it stays in synch with its now distant partner. This implies that these partner particles, even when separated by vast distances, somehow are in constant and instantaneous communication with each other. Meaning, they are not separate things at all, but differentiated portions (or waves) of a continuous unity. Once you create a shared space with another aspect of the Creation, that seeming separation between you and that natural entity diminishes or evaporates. When that occurs, you have entered the Way of Being.

Now, in relation to nature itself, humans have been trained to perceive the matter and energy around them as objective, external stuff that they simply interact with or not. And this alleged reality out there seems all but self-evident. If you walk into a boulder, the debate over whether it is a separate and solid thing rapidly and painfully disappears. Nevertheless, when we look closely enough at the underlying foundation of material existence (energy), it refuses to be neatly categorized according to the same conventions and boundaries that exist at our everyday level of functioning.

Recognizing this, we make two assumptions that underpin the Way of Being:

One: Phenomena are altered (in some sense, even created) by our acts of so-called observation (i.e., participatory consciousness, or blending).

Two: Seemingly separate entities are all interconnected, interrelated, and, ultimately, a composite unity.

This has led some theoretical physicists to suggest that the structure of matter may not exist independently of consciousness itself. While this seems a preposterous notion to most modern noggins, it is a concept long espoused by mystics from many traditions, both ancient and contemporary. As Buddha is purported to have said, "You are what you think . . . having become what you thought." Which is another way of saying that we live in what physicist John Wheeler calls "a participatory universe." Neils Bohr, a revolutionary intellect among physicists, perhaps said this best when he stated, "It is beginning to look like the universe is less and less a great thing and more and more a great idea."

When you soulfully behold a cloud, for instance, you are no longer two separate and distinct entities. Rather, through participatory consciousness, you are creating a shared space in which that cloud and you find interaction and, potentially, communion. It is this participatory consciousness (which I call "blending") that constitutes the modus operandi of the nature mystic seeking the Way of Being.

As the term implies, blending is a way to intimately create and abide in the shared space between you and another element of the natural world. This is the process that Allison employed (Way of Clouds), as described in the preceding chapter. Nature mystics use blending with a panoply of entities and processes, although it tends to be most powerful when relating to something that is part of one's naturality (chapter 9).

Blending involves closely aligning with an aspect of nature, not only through one's consciousness (think soulfulness) but also with one's physiology. Again, Allison used this approach with the cumulus clouds. Others I have guided have blended with wind, water, prairie grasses, trees, mountains, soil, songbirds, rain, waves crashing ashore, snowdrifts . . . the list goes on. They do so by using their posture, movements, facial expressions, gestures and, on occasion, voices to approximate the other entity with which they have created a shared space. So someone blending with the wind may move with it, much as a willow tree might, swaying with the ebbs and flows of the air. In blending with the soil, one might simply lie on it, hold some in one's hands, and *be* with it both in awareness and in form. My good friend Mike is a nature mystic who blends with certain birds by approximating their calls, using the Way of Sound. I have witnessed him engage in this Way of Being many times, often in the depths of a forest or on a seashore. It is mesmerizing.

However, I must interject a caveat. So-called nature mystics who place themselves or others in harm's way by attempting to blend with something dangerously wild (like a big carnivore) are ignoring nature's laws. The dark side of the natural world is not to be ignored or trivialized. The infamous "Grizzly Man" who met his horrific demise by deluding himself into believing he could blend with one of these magnificent and dangerous animals is not to be emulated. With all due respect, such is not the Way of Being. It is the way of being hurt, maimed, or killed. Don't go there.

Method

The Way of Being can be created as follows:

- Identify the focus for your blending. Again, you can simply go into a natural setting and wait to be found in this regard, or you can determine what to blend with in advance. If you're inclined to do the latter but aren't sure what to select, consider your naturality. You may find some clues there.
- Once identified, spend some time soulfully interacting with your "partner" in the Creation. Getting acquainted in this manner will help you to transition to the blending phase. After all, the more you know about this other entity or process, the easier it will be to align yourself with it.
- To the extent possible and reasonable, blend your physiology, including postures, movements, and sounds with this other element of nature. This helps create the shared space that is fundamental to the Way of Being.
- Remember that you are sharing a spiritual space with a "Thou," not an "it." Treat your partner entity accordingly. Ask permission. Give thanks.

Application

The Way of Being is most applicable in these circumstances:

- You have achieved a measure of soulfulness in relation to the natural world and wish to move toward a new level of communion.
- You are seeking to align your consciousness with some attribute in the other entity or process that would help with your spiritual journey. If you seek a greater sense of rootedness and strength, for example, you may want to blend with a tree. If you desire a stronger sense of "flow" and behavioral flexibility, your best nature partner may be water or wind, as examples. Should you wish to experience a stronger sense of élan vital, blending with a waterfall, rain, or (safely) a storm may be in order.

CHAPTER 19

Ways of Transformation

Nature often holds up a mirror so we can see more clearly the ongoing processes of growth, renewal, and transformation in our lives.
—Mary Ann Brussat

If we seek to engage the natural world in our efforts at personal or spiritual transformation, there are a number of "ways" that the Creation provides. Many of these are associated with natural rhythms and cycles, such as the seasons, tides, the transitions between day and night, the movements of celestial bodies, and the phases of the moon, among others. By aligning one's deepest self with one of these cyclical processes, we can create a shared space (as referenced in the Way of Being) that infuses our transformative journey with energy and meaning.

As one might expect, a frequent focus for nature mystics in this regard is the seasons. While spring seems a no-brainer candidate here, in my experience as a nature therapist, I have worked with many seekers who found that winter proved the most helpful ally in their transformational efforts.

In the colder latitudes of our planet, winter is a time of snow, ice, freezing temperatures, and the long sleep of the life force. It is when everything slows down, shuts down, or gets down. I'll explain. Fish slow down. Most of them don't go entirely dormant during the winter, but instead wallow in slow motion, keeping their metabolic rate on ice, quite literally. Animals that hibernate, such as bears or groundhogs, are also in slow-down mode. They ratchet back their metabolism until they are basically in a kind of suspended animation, so to speak. But many plants go into shut down. Slice through the stems of tall prairie grasses in the depths of winter and you'll simply see dry, inanimate matter—what most folks would pronounce "dead." But the plant continues to fully live underground, in its roots. While the life force has retreated far inside, hiding from the frigid air above and the frost in the soil, it remains in stasis, awaiting spring's call.

And then there are those creatures that "get down" with winter. It's a time when they excel. Take wolves, for instance. The snow and cold make tracking prey a snap, and as the rigors of winter exact their toll on other animals, the wolf pack lies in wait for those who fall sick or grow weak. Many herd animals, including buffalo and deer, relish the demise of the bloodsucking insects that torment them throughout the warmer months. But they face the considerable challenge of scrounging enough to eat when their usual fare, mostly fresh vegetation, has all but vanished. And speaking of insects, many succumb to the killing cold, having left behind the seeds of their kind's resurrection when sun and warmth return. But others mimic their larger cousins, like some mammals and reptiles, and essentially hibernate or at least throttle down. Bees, for example, huddle together in their hives, surviving on the collective warmth of the colony. Some caterpillars burrow into thick-layered mats of leaves, essentially cocooning themselves in organic matter. And some insects produce glycerol, a kind or antifreeze that allows them to boost their freeze tolerance level until the warmth returns.

In aggregate, winter is a time of challenge, austere beauty, and quiescence. As such, it offers the nature mystic exposure to the dreamtime of the Creation. Winter is the long sleep, the period when the bright energy of summer and the poignant pageantry of fall have disappeared, leaving a quiet space within which nature can restore itself. Winter, in particular, is the season of mystery. It is the "place" where the life force goes in hiding.

For us, it is the season of death, and that is quite literally true. January has the highest number of human deaths of any month, followed closely by March. February would likely garner second place except it's too short. Nonetheless, winter kills an inordinate amount of animals, including humans, during its harsh tenure. And odd as it may sound, that is the mystery that a nature mystic seeks in the brittle cold and unforgiving winds of winter—to enter a place of darkness, meet one's fears, and then emerge reborn in the spring. Metaphorically and, at times, literally, it becomes the valley of the shadow of death.

For a 50-something physician named Eric, winter became a source for his salvation, not his demise. Gifted and blessed with opportunity, it had taken this man decades to gradually become a burned-out cynic, but he managed to get there. It was not a state of mind to which he had aspired in his younger days. In fact, he had been something of an idealist, fiercely committed to making a positive difference in the world. Well, four years of medical school, another three in residency, and then too much time as a cog in assembly line medicine made long work of that.

"I feel dead inside," he told me.

The man was not a candidate for a few weeks of R&R. He'd done all the "give yourself a break" and self-care stuff that populate glib nostrums on how to fix your life. His exhaustion was not fundamentally psychological, emotional, or even physical. It was spiritual. Until that was addressed, these other avenues for renewal would be all but shut. By the time he graced my door, Eric had been through a handful of therapists, coaches, and healers of various persuasions, but to no avail.

"I've tried a lot of different things, but this nature stuff sounds pretty far out," he told me. "No offense, of course."

"None taken," I replied. "After all, that's what you're here for, right? Cynicism? It's a spiritual disease."

I decided to appeal to his scientific nature. We had some engaging discussions about physics, astrobiology (an earlier interest of his), evolution, animal intelligence, and a host of other nature-oriented topics. Toward the end of our discourse, he shared that he hadn't felt that good in some time, that he truly enjoyed the exchange.

"Glad to hear it. Now, overall, what exactly were we talking about?" I asked him.

He stared back, puzzled, as his intellect tried to concoct the correct answer. Being a cynic, he figured it was a trick question of some kind, so he leapfrogged right over the obvious.

"Well, we talked about a lot of different topics, such as . . . ," he began, but I cut him off.

"Nature," I shot back. "We were talking about nature, and for the first time since I met you, there wasn't any cynicism in your heart. I think we might be on to something here."

As serendipity would have it, early January had arrived and the Midwest was in the clutches of a cold and snowy winter. We agreed to a trek through a lowland prairie, and when we arrived at the trailhead, a brooding overcast filled the sky, whipped along by a stiff and frigid wind, driving the dry snow into small vortexes that skipped over the landscape like whirling dervishes. I loved it.

After we'd put a few hundred yards behind us, Eric's demeanor had returned to an uplifted state, the one he'd displayed during our earlier conversation about the natural world. Nature's capacity to lift our spirits, even after only short periods of exposure (in some studies, no more than five minutes) has been well researched. In my own practice as a nature therapist, I have witnessed this transformation consistently. Even if you feel really bad emotionally, when you're in dialogue with the Creation, you feel bad differently, and in a way that, while not a panacea, is somehow better. Eric proved no exception. But there was more to come than a mood boost. Winter was not done with him.

We sat on a fallen tree next to an iced-over stream and contemplated the stark vista before us. An expanse of reeds and marsh grasses stretched for perhaps a half-mile before ending at a tree line. The stalks were dry, brittle, and washed out to gray or a pale tan. The gusting wind slapped them about rudely, but in a way that, while violent in motion, did no harm. The sky cast a morose and brooding hue, while beneath it the landscape was washed out and asleep, appearing all but lifeless in any traditional sense. After a few moments of silence, Eric stood up, turned a bit away from me and spoke his truth.

"It's just like me . . . or maybe I'm just like it. Either way, when I look out there, I see me," he said, more to the wind than me, it seemed.

"Maybe you'd like to get better acquainted," I suggested.

"I don't know. I already have enough winter inside of me, if you know what I mean. Why would I want more?" he asked.

"Well, I know why but you don't. So instead of me telling you, which you might not believe anyway—being a cynic—why don't you just find out for yourself?" I answered.

He agreed. Over the next several weeks, Eric went out into the winter frequently to engage in soulfulness and to be found. Each time, he returned to visit with me and process his experiences, which he found at times fascinating and, at other junctures, frustrating.

"Sure, it lifts my spirits when I'm out there, but I still come back here to being me," he lamented.

But those short interludes of feeling bad but in a better way were sufficient to keep Eric going out for more. And then, in early March, he asked me to meet him again at that first trailhead. We retraced our steps back toward the creek but more carefully, as the snowpack was melting and pools of slush and layers of rotting ice were everywhere. When we arrived at the fallen tree, he pointed at the nearby creek.

"It's running free now," he said. "The ice is gone."

"What did you learn?" I asked, recognizing something different in his eyes.

"My ice is melting too," he said, a sad smile on his face and a tear in his eye.

Having succeeded in *being with* the winter, Eric was in sync with the season that was now like a brother to him. In its presence and by being with it, he gradually realized that even the seemingly deadest and darkest time gives way to the rebirth of the life force. He discovered, in a felt way rather than an intellectual one, that just as nature has cycles and rhythms, so do we. Soulful contact with the natural world helps us feel and express our own cyclical changes and transformations. Once Eric entered the "current" of nature's slow but rhythmic flow, it began to influence him in profound and seemingly inexplicable ways. In a sense, it carried him along with it. In this instance, it was beginning to awaken his spirit from its long and icy sleep.

All the seasons provide opportunities for us to experience transformational change. However, among them, winter is perhaps the most dramatic, for it begins with dying, waits in apparent death, and then prepares for the coming rebirth. In its own way, it fulfills the Christian narrative of suffering, death, and resurrection, as well as the Hindu and Buddhist belief in reincarnation. As such, it transports us into the most opaque mystery that we contemplate—death and, more directly, one's own death. With the companionship of winter, I have looked my own death in the eye a time or two, and through this season's lessons, I have found my own answer.

Engaging with a season or some other transformational process in nature often requires an extra commitment of time. The kind of synchronicity that Eric was blessed to experience usually necessitates a series of fairly regular nature interactions. Like building a friendship, joining one's psyche and soul with a transformational power and wisdom, like that inherent in a season, requires an investment—of time, of energy, and of will.

Katie, a woman in her early twenties who sought my guidance, provides another salient example. Beset by the struggles around identity and life purpose that are common to young adults, she felt torn between what others (mainly family) wanted her to be and her own murky vision of who she wanted to become. The expectations of others, mixed with her own guilt about "letting people down," were holding her back, and she seemed unable to transition toward becoming her own person.

Employing the nature mystic's practice of being found, she was drawn to the daily cycle of light and dark, of sunrise and sunset. Devising a ritual to further her transformative quest, she arranged her day so that she could "be with" the setting sun each evening and the rising one each dawn. She would sit on a rise in a park next to her apartment building, facing our star, and as it sank below the horizon, she imagined offering it her guilt and the burdensome expectations that fueled it. In doing this, she symbolically breathed these restraining emotions into her cupped hands, outstretched before her, and then released them to the setting sun. At the dawn, in the same place, she would visualize her dream of a "new self," and then reach out toward the sun to "gather" its light and energy, symbolically pulling those back toward and into her heart with her hands.

Gradually, like the journey from night into day, Katie experienced an inner transformation. She felt her old self slowly setting and her new one gradually rising. She was in sync with the transformative power of the Creation, and it was abiding and working within her spirit.

Method

Ways of Transformation can be found in:

- Any naturally occurring cyclical or rhythmic process in the natural world.
- Seasonal changes, including the more subtle ones that take place within each season. Early summer, for instance, is far different than the latter portion of this season.
- The birth, growth, fading, demise, and then rebirth of plants, flowers, and other flora.
- Earth cycles, such as the daily rhythm of dark, dawn, day, dusk, and night.
- Celestial events, such as the phases of the Moon or the voyages of the planets.
- The transformative stages of water as it cycles through the hydrosphere, morphing from liquid to solid (ice), and back again. Water, in particular, is a transformational power in the natural world—one that shapes landscapes, carves rock, and transports floating matter (silt, logs, dried leaves, etc.) over great distances.

Applications

Ways of Transformation are particularly applicable when:

- You feel stuck in your spiritual or existential state.
- You are seeking greater energy and inspiration to support your efforts at personal change and spiritual growth.
- You feel out of sync with nature or life in general.
- You are beset by inner chaos, confusion, or uncertainty, and wonder if life really makes any sense after all.

Chapter 20

The Way of Wild

The clearest way into the universe is through a forest wilderness.
—John Muir

Wilderness is the undiluted expression of the Creator.
—Robert Kennedy, Jr.

We simply need that wild country available to us, even if we never do more than drive to its edge and look in. For it can be a means of reassuring ourselves of our sanity as creatures, a part of the geography of hope.
—Wallace Stegner

Wilderness is sacred.

Unlike settings in the natural world which are closely managed by humans, such as county parks, nature centers, or even state and national forests, a true wilderness preserves a portion of the Creation for "management" by the life force alone. In the wild we encounter the Creator's verve in its purest form on Earth, and we no longer suffer the hubris and presumed mastery of human dominance. It is, then, a place where we experience the humility and awe toward nature that is the wellspring of spiritual experience for the nature mystic.

While it is easy to feel separate from, unaffected by, and dominant over the natural world while in a city, this condescending consciousness ebbs as one moves progressively closer to the wild. In a small town, for instance, nature is more evident and more influential. Its ascendancy increases as one ventures farther from human invention and control, as one leaves the highways and fences, the buildings and concrete, the noise and industrial fumes. This is what many of us seek (albeit often without realizing it) when we head out for the park, the forest preserve, or wildlife refuge—not just respite from the bustle, noise, and odors of so-called civilization, but also to regain a sense of our rightful juxtaposition in the natural order. In wilderness, where the natural rules over the human, we experience ourselves on an equal playing field with the other creatures, forces, and phenomena that comprise the web of life. And if we don't know how to properly and safely behave in the wild, we find ourselves unequal—one down and teetering on the precipice of survival. While collectively we have lost our sense of balance with nature, the wilderness affords individuals the best setting and opportunity to regain it, even if just for a short time.

The Way of Wild is more physically and, at times, spiritually demanding than other paths used by a nature mystic. With very few exceptions, this passageway requires more of a commitment of time and energy than a day hike or an afternoon paddle, let alone a stroll in the local park. It necessitates that one journey into and abide with the embrace of wilderness for several days, or more. For most, this means backpacking, expedition kayaking or canoeing, or mountaineering. As such, it involves a quest, a foray into a reality governed by the Creation in its elemental, unpredictable and, on occasion, unforgiving form.

Which means that whatever cautions and caveats you encountered in reviewing the Way of Storms will be repeated for the Way of Wild. It is a path that the uninitiated should not pursue alone and, even when in the company of the experienced, they should approach it with great respect and considerable preparation. As a wilderness guide reminded a collection of wide-eyed aspiring nature mystics at one of my workshops, "If you don't know what you're doing out there [in the wild], nature will try to kill you." This seemed to let some of the New Age air out of their idealistic balloons, as it should. The so-called dark side of nature is indifferent to the ego's desire to survive, let alone be comfortable or personally fulfilled.

My initiation into the Way of Wild came in the far reaches of Yellowstone Park in the early 1970s. My backpacking companion, Dennis, and I, both novices, had done some of our homework. We had researched and acquired appropriate gear, studied maps, and carefully planned for food, water, first aid, etc. Nevertheless, we hadn't a clue what awaited us, and our choice of Yellowstone as our first venue demonstrated a decided lack of wisdom. Fortunately, the morning we arrived at the trailhead to begin our backpacking foray, fate smiled on us. As we adjusted our gear, we were approached by a 60-something gentleman named Mort who was about to embark on his planned solo pack on the same trail. As it happened, Mort had several decades of backcountry experience under his belt. He asked if he might accompany us and, in one of our wiser decisions, we agreed. A member of a comparatively small contingent who has backpacked the entire length of the Appalachian Trail, Mort quickly began to seem like an angel sent to save our neophyte butts.

Over the next several days, he kindly and gently schooled us in how to find the flow and rhythm that all veteran backpackers seek, and to stay alive and whole in the process. We received instruction in fording streams, selecting a tent spot, securing food from bears, fire starting, meal preparation, water purification, and a plethora of other wilderness necessities. Hiking as we were in early October, we experienced pleasant days, cold nights, and occasional dustings of snow, each of which required adjustments and adaptations. And on our final day in the wild, Mort was there to teach us yet another valuable lesson, albeit an unhappy one.

About eight miles from our exit at the trailhead, this stalwart man stepped on a slick rock while crossing a small stream. His ankle gave way and under the ponderous load of his backpack, he careened off balance and crashed to the ground. The armchair diagnosis was a badly sprained ankle, one on which he could put little weight. The resulting makeshift plan called for Dennis and I to distribute between us as much of Mort's pack load as possible. Hobbled and slowed as he was, this gentleman had no chance of making the trailhead before dark, so I elected to go ahead alone, establish myself there, and be prepared to guide him and Dennis in with a flashlight, as well as render any assistance, which would be far easier once freed of my heavy pack.

An hour later, moving crisply through a stand of towering Douglas Firs and still far from my destination, I sensed eyes upon me. When alone in the wild, it is easy to generate false alarms of this sort, particularly when so inexperienced, but this time my hunch proved correct. Pausing, I swung my gaze to the right where it stopped suddenly, riveted on a large, brown mass about 50 yards off—a grizzly bear. He had long since seen (and probably heard and smelled) me, and I found myself frozen in his steady but inscrutable gaze. The words of the park ranger who had issued our backcountry permit echoed in my brain.

"If you are attacked by a grizzly, drop to the ground and get into the helpless position [curled up in a ball, knees to stomach, hands over the back of the neck] . . . because that's what you are. Helpless."

There are few fears so disconcerting as looking at another creature that is fully capable of killing and consuming you and realizing that, should it elect to do so, there will be little if anything you can muster to stop it. Knowing I could neither outrun a grizzly (which can clock thirty-plus mph on open, rough terrain) nor shimmy up a Douglas Fir, and fearing that any movement on my part, even backing away as is often advised, would provoke an attack, I stood absolutely still save for my heart and lungs. The bear did the same for what seemed a very long time, and then slowly meandered off, apparently not interested in my brand of bipedal protein. I stood statue-like for quite a while, but then managed to begin walking once more and at a very brisk pace, the bear having made me more fleet of foot.

Still wary but feeling the adrenaline easing off a bit, I entered a portion of the trail that tunneled through thick underbrush, largely restricting my sight to immediately ahead and behind. Scrambling along, bent on making time, I was shocked out of my wits by a loud snort followed by heavy thumping and then, with a crash, something large bursting from the dense brush just in front of me. It took my terrified synapses a few moments to make sense of what was happening, but I soon realized that a bull elk had just bolted across my path and, luckily, found it easier to gallop away from rather than over me, which he could easily have accomplished. To a bull elk, moose, or buffalo, a human is a mere speed bump.

Pausing to remove my heart from my throat, I suffered the flip side of the wilderness ecstasy experience—what could be termed, "What was I thinking when I came out here?"

Well, what I was thinking was what it would be like to perch atop a moss-covered boulder on the Sol Duc Trail in Washington's Olympic Peninsula under a painfully deep blue sky, surrounded by a meadow bursting with wildflowers and blueberries, having just emerged naked from an ice-cold lake. Which is where I found myself over thirty years after my close encounters with the bear and elk in Yellowstone. Of the many wilderness events that have transpired for me over the years, most hovered on either end of this pain-pleasure continuum, offering bliss or agony, wonder or dread. And that is the Way of Wild. It is a raw, primitive, elemental, and pure journey into the temple of God, into the divinely inspired ferment of the Creation.

It's not for all of us. In fact, these days it seems only for a few of us, and one could rightfully question our sanity. Nonetheless, the risks are latent with unspeakable rewards. Only in the wild does the nature mystic fully enter the inner sanctum of the Creation.

To finish my tale, I finally made it to the area of the trailhead just as dusk was lowering. Mort and Dennis were, I presumed, miles back, hobbling along slowly. To my dismay, we had misread the trail map. The trail we had followed ended abruptly at the Snake River, and to get to the other side, where our vehicles awaited some ways upstream, we had to ford the fast running waters, and now in the dark. But how? After a quick search up and down stream, I found where a stout rope had been strung across the river at a relatively shallow spot, this to hold onto while making the crossing in what proved to be waist deep water. Placing the less-water-tolerant portions of my gear atop my backpack, I grasped the rope and eased into the current. At its deepest, I was up to my waist, and there was no turning back. Had I turned sideways to the flow, it would likely have knocked me down and swept me off. But the bottom came up gradually, and I made it safely across.

When my companions appeared, long after dark and guided in by my flashlight signals from a bluff overlooking the river, I realized that Mort's crossing would be far more challenging, given his hobbled ankle. Yelling across to each other, we determined that I would hold the rope taught on my end, with Dennis doing the same on the other, this to remove as much slack as possible, giving Mort a better handhold. I positioned my flashlight to illuminate his path over as best it could. He lashed his valuables to the top of his pack, but there was one thorny problem. Mort had with him a walking stick carved from Hickory, one he had used since his youth and which had accompanied him on every backpack of his life. He secured it to the side of his pack, but after he'd waded in up to his waist, it began to break away. Managing to grab it with one hand while holding the rope with the other, he found himself mid-river, wobbling before the relentless surge of the current, trying to save both himself and his beloved walking staff. Catching his gaze in my own, the stark reality of the situation sank in, reflected in his facial expression. It was one of pain, but not from his ankle.

It seemed a timeless pause, but then Mort raised the walking stick up, held it briefly in his gaze, kissed it, and exclaimed, "Good-bye, old friend." And with a flick of his wrist, it was gone. When it was out of sight, he struggled to grasp the vibrating rope with his now free hand, affording the two-fisted grip that the river's indifferent power required. When I helped him climb the bank on my side, there were tears in my eyes, but not his. Dropping his pack, he put a hand on my shoulder.

"It's okay," he assured me. "It's nature's way."

Opening ourselves to the Thou of the Creation, we learn. We are taught. We become students of the life force. And among the many "classrooms" it affords, the Way of Wild is among the most intense and poignant.

While soulfulness certainly is a desirable type of awareness to embrace in the wilderness, a somewhat different manner of consciousness often inhabits those who walk the Way of Wild. Rather than only setting aside specific moments to commune with the Creation, one frequently experiences a kind of unending dialogue in this regard—an interaction that is persistently I-Thou and decidedly real on all levels (physical, emotional, and spiritual).

Words fail me here, but statements like "I walk with the river" and "the sky covers me as I sleep" and "the trees speak" and "the wet, cold, and fatigue hurt, but in a way that makes me more alive"—depict the mindset that envelopes the nature mystic in the wilderness. Most decidedly, the separation between one's self and the rest of the life force grows diffuse and increasingly imperceptible. The illusion of separateness, often hard and fast in the so-called civilized realm, barely covers one's consciousness, and then only like a gossamer veil, easily parted.

Now, just being in the wild is not always sufficient. There are many people who go backpacking or expedition kayaking who are much further removed from a spiritual bond with nature than folks sitting on park benches in Manhattan or tilling flower gardens in Des Moines. The backcountry is bedeviled with its share of "Just do it!" thrill seekers and destination-obsessed overachievers. I have sat beside wilderness trails dozens of miles from the nearest sign of civilization and watched hikers blast right through, barely pausing to notice their surroundings, let alone discover the sanctity of place and moment. Again, for the nature mystic, it is not about being in a place. It is about being *with* a place. And while the place matters, and of the many places one can choose wilderness is among the most exquisite, the more important factor is one's consciousness. Absent one's soulful embrace, no place will invoke the sacred ambiance of the Creation, no matter how magnificent the context.

For those who would journey the Way of Wild but lack the preparation or are otherwise physically compromised, there are alternatives. In fact, there are groups that guide people into the wilderness specifically to bring them into communion with the Creation. If you have the means and the will, consider it. But be wise in your deliberations. Wilderness is under no obligation to suffer our ill-advised presence.

There is little else to say about method or application along the Way of Wild. If one goes into the wilderness to be found, surrounded, and engulfed by the life force, then nature becomes the spiritual guide and teacher. Provided you attend to the bottom rungs on Maslow's Hierarchy of needs (survival first), the consciousness innervating all of Creation will embrace and change you, often in ways that defy expectation. The only hard and fast rule is to be open, to accept this guidance, rather than attempting to "manage" the experience. The wisdom inherent in the wild knows more than that CPU inside your skull.

Virtually every entity and process that one encounters in the wilderness is older, more complete, and more finished than we are. As a young and often misguided species, being in the wild brings us into relationship with life forms and processes that have been evolving for millions (in some cases, hundreds of millions) of years. These manifestations of matter and energy are in balance. Their places in the dance of Creation are perfected in ways that humans have yet to even understand, let alone attain. To enter such a sacred space with the mindset that one will "run the show" is abjectly arrogant.

When in the presence of greater wisdom, don't speak . . . listen.

Listen to the Wild.

Chapter 21

Conclusion

When despair for the world grows in me and I wake in the night at the least sound in fear of what my life and my children's lives may be, I go and lie down where the wood drake rests in his beauty on the water, and the great heron feeds. I come into the peace of wild things who do not tax their lives with forethought of grief. I come into the presence of still water. And I feel above me the day-blind stars waiting with their light. For a time, I rest in the grace of the world, and am free.

—Wendell Berry

People usually consider walking on water or in thin air a miracle. But I think the real miracle is not to walk either on water or in thin air, but to walk on Earth. Every day we are engaged in a miracle which we don't even recognize: a blue sky, white clouds, green leaves, the black, curious eyes of a child—our own two eyes. All is a miracle.

—Thich Nhat Hanh

The memory remains vivid in my mind.

I had pushed and pulled my radio flyer wagon to the edge of a large, viscous mud puddle where our makeshift ballpark's home plate had been. That was before the big rains. After they stopped, our little ball yard in the vacant lot adjacent to my house was a wetland in its own right, at least temporarily. The deluge had dissipated a short time before, but a light mist still wafted through the air. All around was the dripping and running of water. I had to be part of it. A tyke of four and youngest of the family's five progeny, I was often left to my own devices, and I was about to demonstrate why that wasn't always a prudent approach to child rearing.

Scrambling into the bed of the wagon, I stopped to take a furtive sweep of the area to see if any adults or power mad older children were about. Seeing none, I turned to my objective—the muck. I couldn't see it, of course, but I felt a mischievous smile take hold of my face. Opening my raised arms like wings, I closed my eyes, screamed with glee, and leapt forth into the annals of Chard family lore. Shortly thereafter, at the conclusion of repeated vaults into the mud puddle, punctuated by squeals of delight, I appeared at the back door of our house where I was greeted, if that's the right word, by my mother. I was covered head to toe in muddy water and muck.

As one would expect, she was aghast and, once she regained her capacity to speak, admonitions flowed freely from her mouth. But there was something else I saw in her expression. It became a bit more evident when she had me standing up in the washtub in the basement while hosing me down. There was a twinkle in those Irish eyes. In retrospect, that shouldn't have surprised me. Mom was forever outdoors, gardening, hanging the wash, sitting by the lake, shucking corn, and relaxing on the porch swing. She always told us that if we were feeling blue, we should get some dirt under our fingernails, and then we'd feel right as rain. She was salt of the Earth.

In some fashion that she probably couldn't have articulated, Mom completely understood why her four-year-old baby would want to soak himself, through and through, with muddy water and just plain dirt. She recognized, as something did in my own spirit, that I was simply trying to get closer to my other mother—Earth. It should have been clear then that I was not going to be someone who mostly peered out at the natural world through a car window or on a screen saver. My naturality was coming into its own, partly in that mud puddle.

For that, and for what has since followed in my relationship with the Creation, I am most grateful.

So I invite you to venture down your own memory lane in this regard. What are some of your first recollections of nature? Were they tinged with quiet and wonder? Did you burst forth with delight and awe? Were there moments of recoil in fear or pain? Do you remember what it was like to be in that state of childlike fascination, the kind that comes, intuitively, from the part of you that still knows where its existential home resides? How did you first behold one of Creation's doors? And did you ever walk any of its ways, its paths into the mystery? Virtually every person I have ever spoken with has done just that. It is a near universal human experience, and that gives me real hope.

It is through the eyes of a child that the nature mystic seeks to see. It is with those sensitive neophyte fingers that she or he tries to touch the natural world. It is those fresh and wide-open ears that become the portal for listening to the sounds of the Creation. It is the acute sensory perceptions, innocent wonder, and oceanic consciousness of the child that best describe the state of being that a nature mystic embraces.

In those moments when the Creator opens a door to our souls and beckons, we decide.

I bid you to choose wisely.

Embrace nature's ways.

> *Those who dwell among the beauties and mysteries of the Earth are never alone or weary of life.*
>
> —Rachel Carson

INDEX

thinking mind, 26, 70
transcendence, 26, 36-37, 39

U

uncertainty principle, 106-7
universe, 16-18, 70, 84-85, 105-6, 108

W

walking, 74, 76, 98
walking meditation, 76
water, 53-57, 115
Watts, Alan, 14, 25
waves, 25, 107
way of being, 105-10
way of clouds, 101-4
way of night, 94, 97, 99-100
way of place, 34, 39-40
way of sound, 78, 80-81
way of stones, 63-68
way of storms, 89, 92-93
way of transformation, 110, 115

way of trees, 46, 50-52
way of walking, 74-77
way of water, 53-57
way of wild, 116-17, 119-21
way of wind, 69-73
whatever-it-is. *See* life force
Wheeler, John, 108
white noise, 54
Whitman, Walt, 45
Wicca, 86
wilderness, 116-17, 121
wind, 70, 72-73
winter, 83, 110-11, 114
Wood, Bernard, 85

Y

you, types of, 14

Z

Zen, 24

Edwards Brothers,Inc!
Thorofare, NJ 08086
04 March, 2011
BA2011063